New Money:
Staying Rich

New Money:
Staying Rich

Phillip Buchanon

Two Harbors Press, Minneapolis

Two Harbors Press
322 First Avenue N, 5th floor
Minneapolis, MN 55401
612.455.2293
www.TwoHarborsPress.com

ISBN-13: 978-1-63413-174-2
LCCN: 2014919407

Distributed by Itasca Books

Typeset by MK Ross

Printed in the United States of America

CONTENTS

INTRODUCTION

In 2002, I was a twenty-one-year-old kid whose dreams were coming true. I was a student-athlete at the University of Miami, still only a junior, playing Division I football for a nationally ranked team, just like I'd always wanted to do ever since I was ten years old. A year earlier, I was part of a team that went undefeated and won the national championship. I had a taste of glory every Saturday that fall, in front of thousands of screaming college kids and Hurricane alumni boosters. Soon, however, I'd be skipping my senior year and cashing in. Bigger crowds, older fans with more money. I was about to be picked seventeenth in the NFL Draft. One of the few, the chosen, the anointed. I soon would be moving a few thousand miles west from Florida, where I grew up, to California. Oakland would be my new home and the Raiders my new team. And I was ready to raid, or so I thought. Little did I know that being one of the elite lucky ones that got to play professional football would have a dark side that came with it. It wasn't easy to see that all that new money was about to *raid me*. At the time, all I was thinking about was my dream of being a professional athlete finally coming true. I thought the money would be everlasting. I thought I would be set for life: no more worries or family problems.

Getting to the NFL is a long and hard road, from the most talented marquee quarterbacks and wide receivers to the underappreciated linemen and defensive stalwarts. Trust me on this: it's very hard to get someone to pay you to play a game you love. And once you get to the NFL, it's even harder to stay there. The odds are heavily stacked against you.

First, the percentage of high school football players who go to the NFL is .08%. Not even one in a thousand players. For every forty high school football teams, maybe—just maybe—one single player will make it to the pros. If you get promoted to the next level with a college scholarship, your odds improve. I'm not being facetious. Only 1.7% of college players will make it to the NFL. If you make the opening day roster on one of the thirty-two NFL teams, the average career is about three and a half years. If you don't make the opening day roster, it's less than three and a half years. If you're a first-round draft pick, the average career is about nine years.

Now, once you get there, you're facing more hard work and stress. Somebody younger than you wants your job. They're just waiting for you to slip down on the depth chart, or get injured. All it takes is a couple of missed tackles or a sprained ankle. And once you actually get on the field, it's even tougher to stay out there. Again, the odds are in favor of you eventually limping off the field, or worse, getting carried off on a stretcher. This is one very compelling reason why so many athletes choose to leave college early and turn pro. They are justly afraid they will be missing out on a year or two of paydays because expected NFL careers are so short-lived to begin with. The most common injuries are strains, sprains, fractures, dislocations, and concussions. Injuries are relatively common, and they occur on the practice field as well as during games. Injuries are every football player's worst nightmare. More players are "playing in pain" than you ever hear about. If all of us sat on the bench because of minor bruises and sprains, you'd never be able to field a full team.

Pro football players as a whole are terrible money managers. Oh, they earn plenty. They just don't keep it. According to *Sports Illustrated* and ESPN, 78% of NFL players go broke within the first two years of retirement. Many feel lost after the game is gone; they go bankrupt, they get divorced. The documentary *30 for 30: Broke*, a film about the bad decisions athletes make off the field, revealed that NFL players have the lowest salaries, the shortest careers and the worst injury and disability rates in team sports.

I almost became one of those negative statistics, but luckily I found my way after making numerous mistakes. I now dedicate my life to becoming successful off the field. I reinvented myself, beginning an entirely new career. It is not always easy. First, I had to recognize that there was life beyond sports. That's hard for any athlete to deal with. Most of us are young and unschooled in the real challenges we have to face outside the stadium.

Early in my pro career, I spent a lot of time in the Raider locker room with my teammates--veterans with far more experience than I--soaking up stories while soaking in the hot tub. One day before practice, I was warming my muscles in the tub with Jerry Rice, Tim Brown and Rod Woodson. Money, of course, is something we all talked about much of the time. A conversation came up about getting paid for autograph signings. Either Tim or Rod, I can't remember whom, asked Jerry—the most famous of the three—what he got paid to do a signing. Rice said the highest he'd ever been paid was between $150,000 and $200,000.

I was awestruck, in disbelief. I couldn't hold back my response: "Shit, that much? To sign autographs?" Tim laughed at my naiveté. He said, "Man, Bo Jackson got paid $500,000 for an autograph signing." I'd never really understood the expression "my jaw dropped" until that moment, because my jaw did just that. It just dropped and hung there. I was plain shocked.

But I guess if anyone deserved that kind of money for signing his name, few were more deserving than Bo Jackson. As a kid growing up, training to be a professional athlete, I'd always been a fan of Bo, probably one of the greatest all-around athletes we'll ever see. He was the only athlete to be an all-star in two major sports. His career was unfortunately cut short by a hip injury. When I picked up a football, I was Bo Jackson. When I picked up a baseball bat, I was Bo Jackson. And there I was, eleven years later, sitting in a hot tub with three NFL greats, still hoping to be none other than Bo Jackson.

Not a week later, I found myself in another conversation that blew me away all over again. I headed into the locker room to pick up my check, and Rod Woodson was heading out. I called out to him, "Yeah, man, let me see what you're working with. Let me see what that check look like."

"Young buck, you know. It's a couple hundred thousand," he said nonchalantly. There wasn't time for me to question whether he was bullshitting me or not because he pulled out the check and I saw the six digits. The next statement he made stuck with me: "Think about how much money the guy has that wrote this check," he said. "Now that's where the real money is. That's the guy you want to be." It was a short but unforgettable statement.

Driving home that day, I was thinking about a conversation I'd had with a close friend a while back. "Phil, you know you're going to make more money off the field one day than on it," he'd said. At the time I was like, *yeah right*, convinced that the NFL was going to take care of me forever. I had no idea about the failure rate, the injury statistics or how your market value to a team owner can evaporate in an instant while you're aging and sitting on the bench.

But now all I could think about was how he'd been right, and that Rod Woodson was also right. I wanted to be the check writer, the guy whose bank account was so big it could hold my salary, Rod's, and my whole team's.

* * *

The idea for this book came to me during another car ride—this time driving back to Miami after a trip home to Ft. Myers. It was just me, the open road, and my thoughts. No music, nothing but the sound of the breeze for a few hours. I'd turned my cell phone off, even though I could still hear the requests that rang through it all day and night echoing in my head from family and friends: "I need this, I need that, you're supposed to do this for me, that for me . . ." It was all I could think about, and it was driving me crazy. I was lost and I needed help, but I didn't know whom to turn to. The questions were real, and they gnawed at me. Sudden money means you're suddenly faced with a lot of problems (I know that's hard to believe, but trust me, I'll reveal some of them in this book.). How do you do the right thing and still maintain your dignity, your closest relationships, and, most critically, your bank balance at the same time? How do you know when to say yes and when to say no? Who is needy versus who is greedy? Who do you owe for your success, and how much? If you don't care, you don't have any issues or worries. But I cared deeply.

The people who were closest to me, those that I expected to be helpful and understanding of everything I was going through, turned out to be my worst nightmare. A lot of urban families live their dreams through the New Millionaire in the family. This kind of behavior is toxic, affecting the most intimate family ties for life. *Who can I really trust?* was the question I kept asking myself over and over again. It was a harsh reality to finally realize that the people I loved most weren't always the people I could trust. I will always love my family no matter the situation, but in the beginning stages of when I went from having a bank account to a real net worth, I really hated their behavior.

But there was a hidden upside, too. These life-altering moments with my family also taught me a great deal—they made me the dedicated and driven person I am today. Unknowingly, they strengthened my character, changing my personality for the better. You live and you learn, and you realize that the people in your family are just people. For many of them, your money is too tempting not to reach out and grab. You're the one that has to be strong. You're the one that has to set the rules. I just didn't know it yet.

I confided some of my frustrations to a good friend. He suggested that I write a book about what to expect when you suddenly make a lot of money. My aunt, who lives in Miami, has always been in my ear for me to tell my story because a lot of people don't understand the truth. They don't understand the pitfalls one can plummet into when looking to do the right thing because not everyone has the proper resources or wisdom to avoid the deepest ditches.

I want to share my mistakes and my takeaways with those who are New Money Millionaires and and those who aspire to be millionaires.

I'm not just speaking about athletes. There are those that become instantly wealthy, such as lottery winners, or those that inherit unexpected riches. Like athletes, they spent all of their lives focusing on things other than managing money and are suddenly lit up by the prospects of material things. It's hard not to be enticed by the material world when you've spent most of your life scuffling and now there's the boat, the house, the cars—all beckoning to be owned by you.

I want to talk about what I did wrong and what I should have done instead, right from the start. I wish I could have read something like this before I became a New Millionaire.

Just because I've written this book doesn't mean I know everything. I've still got a great deal to learn, but I do think I have relevant experiences to share, a story that can help people in a similar situation to the one I was in. In 2013, I found myself with extra time due to my football injuries, and realized it was the right moment to start writing. As I was taking classes at Miami to finish my degree, I noticed that some of the current football players were in the same position I had been in eleven years before. Two professors I was taking classes with at the university also helped by encouraging me to write this book. They've seen what happened to me happen to another generation of student-athletes.

While I understand that some lessons are learned best through experience, I hope this effort will help you bypass some of the stress, scarred relationships, and most important, the financial burdens I endured when I first came into instant wealth. A wise man once said that making money is easy but keeping it is hard. Let this book be a guide and provide wisdom as you transition through life after becoming a New Millionaire.

My hope is that nobody will have to go through what I went through. My mistakes were hurtful and expensive, and they don't have to happen to you. I've written this book to provide you with a roadmap.

CHAPTER 1

Money Changes Everything

I'm About to Get Paid

I woke up on the morning of April 20, 2002, in my hotel room. "Good morning, papi." I opened my eyes to a beautiful smile. The girl lying next to me was my J-Lo—sexy, sassy, curves in the right places. I was a lucky man. I rolled over and checked my text messages: "Come back to Miami soon, baby, I miss you." That was my Halle Berry. Yes, being a jock means not just two women, but a lot, as many as you can handle. I wasn't trying to be a player; I just had a lot of options. The girls, the groupies, were part of the game. But that particular morning was different, because on that day I became a millionaire, about to see more money than most kids from my old neighborhood would see in their entire lives.

The Oakland Raiders had just selected me to play cornerback in the first round, seventeenth overall draft pick of the 2002 NFL Draft. I was a member of the elite class of that year's prospects.

Newborn Millionaire [nü-bôrn mi(l)-yə-'ner] ▶ *n.*
1. Synonymous with **New Money Millionaire** and **New Millionaire.**
2. One who goes from being broke to being a millionaire overnight.
3. One who becomes the CEO of a corporation before he or she is ready to do the job (Young Silicon Valley Multimillionaires).

4. Someone who comes into their fortune with undeveloped instincts for how to assess people's real motivations and interest in them; ill-prepared for the shark attacks.

Money came to me overnight, and I would never be the same person again. It felt good to send a text to my agent's contact: "I got you on those loans." In the months leading up to the draft, I had already spent close to a million dollars. Now I could repay the open line of credit that had been given to me. Yes, all borrowed knowing there was a pot at the end of the rainbow. It was a relief to go from being in the red to being in the black, from having debt to having it all. It was something I had always dreamed of; something I knew was coming from the beginning, something you could even say I spoke into existence.

In retrospect, it seems a little strange. Once you cross the bridge of receiving this type of money or attention, people look at you differently. They look at you in a good way when everything is going well, but they also look at you in a stupid way when things go badly. So you have to understand what you are signing up for because you will be forever judged.

When I was a kid, I thought a hundred dollars was a lot of money. I thought that meant you were rich and your life would be forever changed, but I didn't know any better because I was just a kid. I never understood the value of a dollar back then. Now, twelve or fourteen years later, a million dollars to me was like that movie *Blank Check*. I was Macaulay Culkin in the film *Richie Rich*. I thought I could get anything or do anything.

The craziest thing about being a millionaire is that once you spend that first dollar, you are no longer a millionaire.

The day of the draft, I remember rolling up to the gas station in my black-and-silver, two-toned Cadillac Escalade to buy a Pay Day candy bar, something I had done since age nine, with hopes that one day I would have a real payday.

When the Raiders called my name, I could not really enjoy the moment because of the mixed emotions I was feeling. I had received a lot of phone calls from the teams that were picking fifth through twelfth in the draft, but they chose to go in a different direction. One of my college teammates, Clinton Portis, texted me and said, "Well, you ain't going in the top ten ha ha ha." I didn't mind the comment. But all I could think about was not getting that Bentley anymore. Oh well.

Becoming a first-round draft pick was everything I imagined it to be; however, the reality wasn't something I was prepared for.

I was ready for the NFL, but I sure wasn't ready for life off the field. I wasn't prepared to deal with how my family and friends would react to me becoming the new richest kid on the block. I felt the tension at home right away. There were a lot of negative vibes coming from my mother and certain other family members. They felt that I picked the wrong agent. They said if I chose the agent that they wanted (he told them he had a lot of connections with a lot of NFL teams), I would have gone higher in the draft and made a lot more money. Perhaps so, but if I made double the money, my problems would have likely doubled as well.

I didn't know how to spend my money properly; I just knew how to keep spending and spending. I wasn't prepared for any of it. Damn, if only I knew then what I know now.

All Good in the Hood

I'd been getting paid for a long time for what I did on the field, but not like this, not like in the NFL.

After the sudden flush of being rich began wearing off, I began to reflect on just what had happened in my life. You know how this is. You run the tape back and begin reviewing the highlights (as well as the lowlights).

It was very difficult to do what I did, because the odds of becoming a drug dealer were a lot better than of making it to the NFL. My mother's new husband was in the armed forces, and I forced to live in Charleston, South Carolina for about a year and a half. After moving back to Ft. Myers, Florida from Charleston, I was placed in ESE (for students who are learning disabled) at Pelican Elementary School. This was embarrassing because I knew that wasn't true. I couldn't understand why they wouldn't give me a fair chance in the classroom. My mom and dad didn't worry about this at the time because me being at school was better than me being in the streets.

*   *   *

I was all but mute as a kid growing up in Ft. Myers. I didn't say a whole lot, because I was all about working hard by showing and not telling what I was going to do. Ft. Myers was all I really knew. Thomas Edison and Henry Ford both spent winters there, but certainly in much nicer neighborhoods than where I grew up. Everything started for me in an area named the Battle Homes, a subdivision where I spent most of my time. I was at my grandmother's house a lot. My grandmother lived in a single-family house in the Battle Homes on Meadowview Circle. The house was originally a three-bedroom house, but my family converted it into a four-bedroom house. My grandmother used the garage as a room. At one point, there were as many as a dozen people living there.

It was in that was where my Uncle Two-Face began teaching me baseball and football when I was about six years old.

My mother finally moved us out of my grandmother's house and into an apartment, but that didn't last long. We ended up bouncing around from place to place until we finally settled down in a house on Bert Drive. This house was a two-bedroom with a den. I lived here until my senior year in high school. When I got sick, I would go in the backyard and pick out fresh oranges and grapefruits from the trees.

I marked the distances of forty and sixty yards on the road in front of the house to serve as my training ground. The forty yards was for football and the sixty yards was for baseball. I took advantage of my strategic location. Bert Drive was in the center of everything I could do in Ft. Myers. It was only a ten or fifteen-minute walk to the projects—Sable Palms (aka "Buck Town"), Michigan Court and Palmetto Court. I had a cousin and some friends living there. My favorite local store, Joe Lias, was only a couple of minutes away, and that is where I would buy my milk and cookies or snacks.

When I got to my adolescent years, I spent a lot of time at the Stars Complex, a Ft. Myers sports facility where I began honing my baseball and basketball skills. There I met a lot of young kids like me, some that aspired to be serious athletes and others that didn't.

Deion Sanders's grandmother was living across the street from the Stars Complex. I remember when my baseball teammate, Prentice Harris, invited me over to her house when we played for the Dunbar Indians. I seem to recall that the house was green and white—like the color of money—and it made me feel special.

But when I finally stepped into Deion's mother's house in the Gateway area, close to Lehigh Acres, Florida, I knew I was going to make it as an athlete. It just gave me that feeling. Every time I saw Deion's mother's house, it motivated me. I felt like I could just reach out and touch my coming success. As a kid, if I felt a connection from a person after shaking his hand, I felt like I had a great chance of getting what they had. Today, I still feel that way.

My cousin was a bad influence. I'd hang around the projects with him and be a part of his petty-theft schemes. It didn't take long for me to understand that this was not the road to where I wanted to go. I took my training to another level on Bert Drive. On school nights, I stayed up late and often worked out at midnight or 1:00 AM. I didn't want anybody to see me training.

I would walk to the Stars Complex, borrow a bike (which is sort of like stealing to a certain degree, but I rationalized it by saying it was for a good cause: my budding athletic career) or someone would give me a ride. I never missed a chance to play basketball or baseball there. Competition was in my blood.

The walk there, if I had to, was like an hour, so on the way I would throw rocks for fun or race through hidden paths like I was breaking away for a long run in football. Sometimes I had to cut through the cemetery to go to the complex. It was a little scary at night, but that never stopped me.

I always felt like I was destined to do big things in my life. It was like that movie *The Truman Show*. Why? I have no idea. It was like there was someone watching over me to make sure I did the right things. This was a weird feeling I had from time to time. I would see shooting stars at night and make a wish as I was walking or riding a borrowed bike home from the Stars Complex. Maybe it was somewhat spiritual. Maybe I felt blessed. Anyway, I just knew.

*   *   *

In the streets, all I heard about was fast money. Most of the men in my family were around drugs. My Uncle Curtis was sort of a role model because he was the dominant man in our house. And he was a drug dealer. I know this sounds strange, but he had a lot of good qualities that I admired, such as taking care of our family. After Uncle Curtis died, I could have started doing the stuff that he was doing—and it was tempting because my family never struggled when he was alive. Or at least that's what my family kept telling me.

My Uncle Two-Face kept me in line because he wanted to change that trend. He was doing what Uncle Curtis told him to do, I guess. Or maybe I would have been working at a fast-food restaurant like McDonald's, or in and out of jail. There were a lot of paths I could have taken. I was a young kid, and all I wanted to do was help my family.

I had a pretty good work ethic early on. I was on the Dunbar Little League All-Star team that had all black kids. One game I remember clearly: we were playing against the North Fort Myers All-Star team, and they were predominately white. I went 3-for-4 against Cory Hockinson, a right-handed pitcher, whom I heard was selected for the junior national team. After we lost the game, my coaches were talking to us in the dugout, when a few of the other team's dads came over. They asked to see me. They told me how well I played that day. Their last words were about me having to continue working hard because they thought I had talent. They thought I would go places. That motivated me even more as an athlete. I decided I'd take their advice. This fed my ego, but more importantly, it motivated me to work harder and improve my skills.

Looking back, I saw that people treated me well as soon as I was identified as an elite athlete. This happened one afternoon after racking up five touchdowns in one game for the Riverdale Wildcats, the Pop Warner football team in my neighborhood. First play of the game, 80 series, the quarterback performed a five-step drop before launching the ball into the air for me to track down and get in the end zone. It was a guaranteed touchdown; first play of every game. I was just plain faster than almost anyone my age. After the games, people would come up to me and congratulate me. Some started as strangers that grew into familiar faces week in and week out. "Man, you really helped me out today, Phillip," one guy casually mentioned. This meant that he was gambling on the game, and I made some big plays for him to win his bet. The comment was followed by a thick handshake before putting my hand back in my pocket.

I was actually good enough to have a shot at making it as a Major League Baseball player. While I was in high school I turned down a $500,000 signing bonus to play with the Cincinnati Reds. I missed my last year of high school baseball because of a wrist injury that occurred while I was on the basketball team. I wore a cast from my wrist to my armpit. I injured some small bones in my wrist, but I kept playing because the team needed me.

Even though I said no to the money, I walked around high school feeling like I was a millionaire. Half a million was half of the dream. So I stopped accepting the Reds' phone calls. But my mother didn't. She kept talking to them, and continued to persuade me to take the deal. The main reason I didn't take the deal was because I was in love with football. At first, the Reds only wanted me to play baseball, but I still wanted to play football. Bo Jackson was a two-sport man, and I thought I could be, too. The Reds came back and said I could do both.

The other problem was how hard I'd have to work. Believe it or not, the one-day workout was longer than any other workout that I ever had up until that point. I didn't expect that they would be all-day affairs—like eight hours long. I thought the Reds would have me hit and field balls, and then, after a couple of hours, I would be off to the showers. I never knew that you could play that much baseball in one day. I had to hit for three or four hours, and started getting blisters on my hands. On top of that, I practiced fielding and situational baseball drills. It felt like a nine-to-five job. I never envisioned practice being like that.

And, of course, my mother and grandmother talked about what they were going to buy with my money. I quickly realized baseball wouldn't be enough. I thought to myself that I would have been playing for free between their houses, cars, shopping sprees, and traveling. I wasn't ready for my free time and summer to be over before I went to the University of Miami. In all honesty, there was too much going on, and I needed some real help. I didn't want to go through all those workouts for $500,000.

When people from the hood identify young talent, they want to see you become successful. The opportunities to get out of the hood were so few that the entire community took great pride when someone made it big or even showed the promise of making it big. I was someone who was expected to make it, so people in the hood looked out for me. No one tried to bring me down. They showed me love and protected me. I assumed that once I became a New Money Millionaire, the advice would still remain genuine. I figured money would just bring better advice, a better life. But what I didn't know was how all this would just bring me some tough life lessons.

Money, the Problem Solver

I thought everything was going to be so much easier. I grew up on the philosophy, "If you're going to have problems, you might as well have problems with money." I thought money was a safe haven. That's what I'd been taught from a young age. When I was about seven or eight, I remember sitting on the floor of my Uncle Curtis's living room watching *Rambo* as people walked in and out of the house. Everyone greeted me: "Hey, sweetheart," "Hello, honey," "Hey, Phillip." Sometimes these were family members saying hello, but mostly they were women who knew my uncle. The difference between the two was the length of their stay. My family members would be in and out, but I'd be halfway through *Rambo* before a woman would leave. "It was good seeing you again. Your uncle is a good man. Keep up with your grades, okay?" she'd say as she went out the door. I'd say okay, annoyed that she was talking to me right at my favorite part when Rambo messes up the dog that the cops sent in to find him.

"Phillip, you ever see money like this before?" Uncle Curtis asked.

He would pull out a roll of bills that was held together with a green rubber band, "Nah," I'd shrug.

"That's okay, you're going to make it one day and have a stack bigger than this."

My Uncle Curtis got stabbed to death when I was around eight or nine. I was getting ready to play my first year of full-contact football, and he was murdered before that could happen. He wasn't a bad guy; he just chose a bad profession. He was big on picking up kids to play football to keep them off the streets.

He was someone I respected as a father figure. I remember one particular time my mother dropped me off at my grandmother's house so she could run the street. I was a mama's boy back then. But what my Uncle Curtis told me that day is something that I will always remember. When I was crying after watching my mother sneak out of the house, he said, "Listen to me and stop crying; from now on you are going to be around me and your other uncles. No more crying like a little girl, you are a man now. No more hanging on or chasing your mother, okay?"

I literally did a 180 and started carrying myself like a young man. I loved being around my Uncle Curtis at that time. I learned three things: to be tough, not to cry like a little girl, and that I was going to make it in sports.

I don't know what made him so confident, but I believed it. Maybe he said it because he didn't want me to go down the same path he did. Money solved family problems. Everybody in my family looked up to him. When he died, those are the things that stuck with me. I was young, but I remember his body builder physique and his Jheri curl, like from the movie *Coming to America*—the Soul Glo commercial.

Uncle Curtis died not long after he first introduced me to his green rubber band, but it wasn't the last time I heard about that stack of money. "Man, if Uncle Curtis was still here, everything would be okay." That's all I heard from my family members. That, or about the money problems they had. From a young age, it was ingrained in me that money was the problem solver. Maybe if Uncle Curtis was still alive he could have enlightened me as to how to preserve money and have sound financial management. Regrettably, I had to learn the hard way—from the school of hard knocks.

Once I signed my first contract in 2002, problems that seemed so monumental before were a lot easier to digest. This is what Uncle Curtis was talking about. I no longer had to take a deep look into the problem and figure out a solution that fit within my means. My answer to the problem—any problem—was money. Whether it was family members that found themselves in a bad financial situation, or if the problem was not having enough bottles of Cristal at my table in a nightclub, my money would be there, and everyone knew it.

Bank Buchanon

When you are blind to the little things, you end up creating monsters. People thought I should play Santa Claus and pass out money like it was candy on Halloween—$500 here for a family member, $1,000 there for a friend. I even had someone I didn't know come up to me and say, "I need some help, so your mother told me to ask you." A neighborhood friend that lived down the street from my grandmother claimed to have made a verbal agreement with me on the playground when I was a little kid for $1 million and came to cash in when he heard I signed a contract.

I kept making withdrawals from Bank of America, while the whole city of Ft. Myers was cashing checks that I'd signed at Bank Buchanon. The problem was that they were only making withdrawals, never depositing anything back. No bank can stay in business operating like that. Bank Buchanon had to stop, drop and shut down. I needed to protect the end zone.

Superman Syndrome

I didn't help the situation, either. By my junior year of college, I started spending like I could already count on that million. How much was I worth at twenty years old? I was valued at millions of dollars after a strong spring football showing during practices. Leading into my junior year during spring football, I signed an insurance policy with Lloyd's of London. I eventually had to pay back the premium—it was more than $8,000 but less than $15,000—after I signed my NFL contract. This is standard procedure with all of the top college football players.

As a student-athlete, we received a monthly check to cover room and board and used the little that was left over for essentials. Every month, I practiced my autograph when Ms. Dorothy from the business office made me sign for my check. Next, I walked to the Bank of America across the street. "I'll take this in all five and one-dollar bills please," I'd say to the teller. Then I'd slide the green rubber band from my wrist and wrap it around my cash, just as my Uncle Curtis had done. I was continuing a legacy, and I felt proud of it. My roll wasn't as big as my uncle's yet, but I knew it would be eventually.

At that point, I kept no money in my checking account. I had no savings, no bonds. Nothing. I cashed that check for the three and half years I was at the University of Miami. If I would have known about cash-advance companies or similar financial institutions in those days, it would have been on and poppin'. I would have spent my monthly check before I even got it. In short, I knew next to nothing about money.

After I cashed my check, I'd catch a ride with an upperclassmen and head straight to the Dadeland Mall. I had to make sure my kicks were on point, so I'd swing by Foot Locker. By the end of 2001 I had about forty or fifty pairs of sneakers—Jordans, Air Max's, or whatever shoes I wanted at the time. All of my money was being spent on nice clothing like collared shirts, slacks and fancy athletic apparel. Having good shoes back then was like having a nice car with flashy rims. It also meant having your own personal VIP section at a club. You're the man, and the more people that convince you that you are, the bigger your ego gets. Egos, of course, grow faster than bank accounts, and you quickly find out that it is hard for the money to keep up with the ego.

I was a regular at Macy's. "Phillip, we just got these new Tommy Hilfiger shirts in. Check 'em out," the salesman, who knew me by name, would call out the second I walked in the door. The salesmen would always pump me up by feeding my self-image with phrases like, "What's up, superstar?" or he would call me "big timer" or "big money." It's so funny because I don't remember the names of any of the people who wanted me to spend my money with them. I got what I wanted, and they got my money, so I guess it was a fair trade off, right? We were the new kids on the block at that time, and I felt like I was the shit. My swag was at an all-time high. The more we kept winning at Miami, the better it got at retail outlets.

In a matter of hours, the check that was supposed to feed me paid for condoms, replaced my old toothbrush, and paid for my friends and I to go out for pizza. I spent everything. This may be a great country, but let's be real: we're known throughout the rest of the world for our consumerism. We are congenital spenders. And so, in the spirit of American spending, I did what every other good student-athlete did: spend, spend, spend.

Until I went broke. At least I looked good broke.

Superman Syndrome [sü-pər-man sin-drōm] ▶ *n.*
1. Belief that one is so strong that he or she can stand up to anyone, at any time.
2. Puffing up one's chest to match one's ego.
3. Characterized by flying girls out every weekend, hitting the clubs multiple times a week, having four or five cars in your name and the motto, "If you can't pop tags, it's not worth wearing." (Meaning it had to be brand new before I could even think about putting on any shirt.)
4. Of, or pertaining to, Phillip Buchanon during his New Money Millionaire phase

The check that Ms. Dorothy handed me when I started college was just the beginning of my Superman Syndrome. The severe symptoms started during my junior year in college. As I got closer to my NFL payday, my symptoms worsened. I had celebrity status, more

Lois Lane's than I could count or remember, and soon I'd have a hell of a lot of money. I felt invincible. In my mind, I could do what I wanted, buy what I wanted and go where I wanted with whomever I wanted. Fast money fooled me because my family had made me believe what pop culture confirmed, which was that when I got my money right I could do anything. Once I got my money, you couldn't tell me a damn thing. Stop talking to me; everything sounded like Spanish and I just didn't want to hear everyone's shit.

I already had the seed of superpowers on the field, now all I needed was the cash to make those superpowers blast off. Once I got my money, you couldn't tell me there was a girl I could not have or a day of boredom I couldn't solve. Money was the medicine that cured the boredom disease. Hell, you could fix monotony very easily with Jet Skis or a shift in time zone—a little trip to the Cayman Islands or Belize.

What I hadn't met yet was my Kryptonite, but that would come soon, in the shape of financial instability. Money might be great, but if you're not careful it doesn't last forever. It slips away at different speeds, and it does this sneakily, hoping you do not notice, until one day you finally . . . well, notice. Then, you're dead broke.

A Safety Net with a Hole in the Bottom

My first year in the NFL I was a newborn baby. My whole world was new, and survival would be near impossible without help. But, also much like a newborn baby, there was an influx of people seemingly willing to help me (or help themselves) until it came time for cleaning up a mess or a smelly diaper. People cooed, oohed, and aahed; the fans were great, and the large numbers of available women made me feel like a Beatle or a member of a boy band. I remember one fan even cried when she met me.

I think I woke up after all the fun I had with women. Dealing with women is difficult because at some point you begin wondering whether they want you for you or for your money. Big distinction there. Your personality is defined by the size of your bankroll, at least while you're out with the ladies. I knew I had to do better by trying to find the right help. When I was with the Oakland Raiders, I didn't have a mentor to lean on during certain difficult situations. I was still very young, eager, but I had a lot to learn.

In Oakland we had a lot of superstars, so everybody was doing their own thing. You had to look out for yourself because those veterans were on a different level. At the University of Miami, it was different. We worked together as a team, even though there were a lot of talented players. In a college locker room is a brotherhood; in the pros, it's all about business. Looking back, I probably should have been more single-minded and looked out for myself. My family was not helping me, so the responsibility of looking out for myself totally fell on me.

When you're new to things, you do stupid things. I was doing what I felt was right; I had no clue how to transition my lifestyle into being around millions of dollars. I didn't have a system or a plan. I just spent money at will on whatever I wanted at any given moment. Shoes and clothes, slam it. Jewelry, slam it. Partying with women, slam it. Trips to the islands at a moment's notice, slam it.

Another thing new money has in common with newborn babies is that it doesn't come with an instruction manual. Money can be very clever, can't it? Everywhere I turned, I was meeting new people that had the same number of zeros before the decimal place in their bank account as I did, so I turned to them for advice. But I was going about it the wrong way. I was asking people who didn't know any better than I did. It's like asking the guy next to you in class to help you with your homework because you didn't understand a concept taught in class. You think he's smarter than you, but he's probably not. Better to just ask the professor during his office hours, wouldn't you think? The thing I wasn't doing was distinguishing between Newborn Millionaires and Self-Made Millionaires.

At some point, I realized I needed some advice.

Self-Made Millionaire [self-mād mi(l)-yə-ner] ▶ *n.*

1. One who starts from zero and gradually transitions from having no money to becoming a prodigious accumulator of wealth through arduous work efforts, dedication, ability, fiscal responsibility, and a little luck.
2. Understands the meaning of the dollar rather than just spending it.
3. Millionaire status, in this case, is stable and sustainable.
4. Of, or pertaining to, Bill Gates, Sara Blakely, Puff Daddy, 50 Cent, Warren Buffet, Dr. Dre, and Oprah.

What I first failed to realize is that self-made millionaires *remain* millionaires, and sometimes become billionaires, because they learn to invest wisely and manage their money. I missed that piece of the equation. While the self-made millionaires were calculating how to *grow* their money, I was calculating how to *blow* my money. They had accumulated wealth over time and had experience in managing their finances, often with expert help. But they largely had to learn enough about finance to understand when they were getting solid, reliable advice instead of a broker-pretender who only wanted to (legally) skim their account. I didn't think about any of that. I was just trying to match my peers, to spend as much as they did—keeping up with the Joneses. Because I did not distinguish between Newborn Millionaires and Self-Made Millionaires, I was following the lead of many who had come into money no sooner than I.

What is clear to me now is that the majority of New Money Millionaires were spending just as blindly as I; it was the blind leading the blind.

CHAPTER 2

Living Beyond Your Means

Live like a king now, or a prince forever.

—Bart Scott, former Pro Bowl linebacker
for the New York Jets

In the end, after you've had your fun, after the last call comes and goes, and the lights are shut down, and you're feeling fine, let's take a look at your bank account. How are you going to feel when you wake up in the morning a little less rich? Yes, that's the critical question. But there are others I'd like to ask you, too. Will you be okay with your balance once the bill from the strip club posts on your credit card bill? Did you save more than you spent? Will you still respect yourself when the hangover wears off? Here, I reference strip club, but you can substitute anything that relates to your lifestyle: country club, comedy club, yacht club, nightclub . . . you get the idea. These are all places where it's easy to live beyond your means.

For Newborn Millionaires, there is a huge risk of living too large. Suddenly, you're in a world where the cash is always flowing, where you have access to parties you only dreamed about before, and you start hanging out with people you only knew through the tabloids. Deals, discounts, and freebies abound because, ironically, the more money you have, the more things you get for free. The grounded celebrities, who are secure in their own skin, don't think much about the freebies because they are used to it; the greedy types expect the swag bag to be on their doorstep before they agree to get out of bed. But now I understand it. Okay, if I'm wearing your brand on the red carpet, I'm giving you free advertising when it hits the press. It's a good deal for both of us.

I remember when my new wealth and status started opening doors. I was invited to parties where there were rappers and movie stars—real VIPs, not pretenders. I'd walk in and think, *these are the people I idolized as a kid, and now here I am*. It was difficult not to let this feeling go to my head.

One event I attended early on was Kelly Rowland's birthday party in L.A. Rowland was a singer in Destiny's Child before Beyoncé became Beyoncé. I brought my college teammate, Clinton Portis, who was playing for the Washington Redskins at the time, along with me. As we headed to Lucky Strike, the bowling alley / nightclub, I wondered who else might be there. I counted on seeing Beyoncé and Destiny's Child's Michelle Williams, of course. The list didn't stop there, though. As it turned out, Serena Williams, Outkast, and Jay-Z were there. It was celebrity-packed, A-listers only. How did I get invited? I knew the birthday girl. When I arrived, Kelly came up to greet me. I was a good friend of her brother, Lonny, so I'd gone to some of these parties before. I didn't mind being his wingman.

But this time, I felt different. Now, I was there on my own. I thought I belonged on my own merit as a budding celebrity. Clinton saw Kelly and me, and he playfully gave me a hard time, thinking I was holding out on him about my relationship with her. I tried to tell him we were only friends, and just as I was explaining it, our conversation was interrupted by Jay-Z, who'd come over to where we were standing in a more secluded area in the back. Jay-Z and I just talked about sports and business, and we kept it mostly casual. Often when you go to a party and you don't know too many people, famous or otherwise, you can feel like an outsider. I felt like I belonged.

Another time, I was in Vegas waiting for an elevator in my hotel when a guy stopped me and asked, "Aren't you Phillip Buchanon?" I shook his hand, and he immediately extended an invitation to Puff Daddy's party. He was connected to the Michael Jackson dynasty somehow and, of course, was invited to the party. Because he was an Oakland Raiders fan, and I was on the team, I was invited, too. I went upstairs to my room to clean up and met him and Michael's father, Joe Jackson, downstairs in the lobby a few minutes later. Outside the hotel, there was a town car waiting for us, ready to take us to the party.

Once we got there, I followed my new friend and Jackson around until we got to a door with a big black security guard standing at the entrance. It was clear that the bodyguard knew Joe, because he cracked a smile, said "What's up?" and let us in. I didn't expect the room to be as big as it was; when I walked in, the entire place must have been at least 15,000 square feet. I looked around, and the first person I noticed was Bruce Willis. Immediately, scenes from *Die Hard* started flashing in my mind. I shook his hand, and he offered me a shot as a waiter walked past with a tray. He was echoing Puff Daddy, encouraging everyone to get his or her drink on. It was rumored that Michael Jackson was upstairs, but I never saw him. Either people were lying, or he just wasn't in the mood to socialize. People were drinking and dancing; I was standing in the back, soaking it all in.

Actually, I was trying to play it cool. That's why I declined Bruce's shot earlier; I needed to make sure I kept a low profile. Most of the parties I attended were also populated by athletes, mainly football players I knew or played with. This was a new world. The great majority of pro athletes have financial status, somewhere between very well off and wealthy, but very few are real celebrities. A celebrity athlete is doing commercials and is famous beyond his sport. Peyton Manning, Tom Brady, Derek Jeter. Those guys are celebrities. I couldn't help but feel excited. It's not every day you're in a room with Bruce Willis and Puff Daddy. I didn't want the memory clouded by drinking.

Then there was the free stuff. As soon as I became a New Money Millionaire, the free stuff started pouring in like maple syrup on pancakes. I thought free stuff was for people in need. I guess not. At one point, I had three free phones—two from Sprint and one from Verizon. I was driving two Hummers and a Cadillac, free of charge. At one point in 2007, I was also offered a loaner Rolls-Royce Phantom. I had just re-signed with the Tampa Bay Buccaneers. Unfortunately, I had to turn down the Phantom because there just wasn't enough room in my garage; the thing was huge. I just had too much stuff. There is a movie, Funny People, starring Adam Sandler, and his character is a famous, successful stand-up comic. There's a scene where he goes into his cluttered garage, full of all kinds of unused stuff—all freebies—and he muses about how illogical all of it is. That's what my garage looked like. Can you imagine refusing a Rolls? I was heartbroken at the time, though that is not a feeling that should evoke any sympathy. It reminded me that part of what comes with success or even modest celebrity-status means that people will always have motives when they give you something. They want something in return—maybe not right away, but someday. There's no such thing as a free lunch.

I had VIP access to concerts and award shows, not to mention great seats at the Mike Tyson fight in Washington, DC in June 2005, when he was up against Kevin McBride. This was leading into my first season for the Houston Texans after I was traded from the Oakland Raiders. On the way to the fight, our foursome was composed of ex–University of Miami players Clinton Portis, Andre Johnson, Santana Moss, and me. We rode over to the arena in a Rolls-Royce, a Bentley, and a Maybach. We switched cars as we drove into the arena, again before the after-party, then one last time on our way back to Clinton's house in Virginia.

If I walked into a trendy restaurant with an hour-long wait at the door, there was somehow a table just getting cleaned off with my name on it. I was privileged even for something simple, like getting my teeth cleaned. I had my choice of appointments, even if the dentist office's schedule was full.

I wasn't getting free stuff because I was a charity case; I was getting free stuff because I was helping companies brand their products. If people could say, "I saw Phillip Buchanon wearing *X* last week," it was worth it for the company. I wasn't getting the leftovers, which is often what people in need are left with. I was getting it all hot and fresh. It's not to say that I couldn't afford some of this stuff on my own, but often I didn't have time to consider whether I could afford the freebies or even wanted them because they were in my hands before I could think. When you analyze why wealthy people give to charity, it's very simple: 1) they need the tax deduction, 2) they feel guilty because they're wealthy and need a cause, and 3) it makes them feel good to help others. Call me cynical, but I'll bet the first two reasons are the prime motivators. The last one is a third-and-long.

The thing is, it's all show. So much of this lifestyle is rented, and there's always a return date attached. All of it is just a really nice paint job. It's like designers giving an actress a gown to go to the Academy Awards. If you're a megastar, you probably get to keep the dress; everyone else is borrowing. All the women at home are sitting on their couches, glued to the red carpet preshow, dreaming of one day wearing the designer dress their favorite stars are showcasing. These red carpet shows, in case you didn't know, are all scripted. The interviewers are asking planted questions to make sure the viewing world knows exactly what designer dress your favorite star is wearing. What most people don't realize is that the next day when the makeup has been removed and the hair is let down, the dress goes back in the garment bag and gets returned to the designer.

It's all show. It was the same with me. If someone complimented me on the Hummer I was driving, it was much easier to say "Thanks" than to say "Thanks, it's nice of the dealership to let me drive it for free."

There was a huge gap between what I really had and what it seemed like I had. I started to come to certain realizations—about how much of an impact pop culture had on my life, how much it played on my desire to have more money so I could live like the rappers and actors I watched on BET. If you're a black athlete who has come into money and left the neighborhood, you're still getting your cultural cues from BET. You watch those stars on TV at a young age, and you want to become them. It's part of the fantasy of the American dream. Why do you think there are so many reality and celebrity shows on TV? They sell the image, and the image sells the products. Once I stepped into the world of celebrity, however, I realized that who I once dreamed of becoming, the clothes I had once dreamed of wearing, and the cars I had once dreamed of driving, didn't always reflect the amount of money in a person's bank account. I heard so many stories from athletes and show-business entourages about how some well-known personality was close to being broke and just flashing for show. In short, they needed the world to think they had money to look good. They needed to impress everyone with a façade. Money for show.

Every time I heard one of those stories I filed it away as a life lesson: don't become that person. If their downhill stories weren't enough, my own situation certainly was. The free stuff makes you think you're driving a car you can afford and wearing clothes you paid for. But that just isn't true.

Suddenly, I was looking to buy a house with a four-car garage just to fit the four cars I wasn't paying for. It doesn't take too long to say, "What's wrong with this picture?"

I was in the perfect position to live beyond my means, but I was in way over my head.

Getting Out of My Lane

It's sort of like driving on the highway. Sometimes you see the Ford Pinto trying to keep up with the Mercedes-Benz. It looks sporty and sounds sporty, but as soon as it hits a certain speed, the Pinto begins to shake. As Herman Edwards put it in *30 for 30: Broke*, "You've got champagne taste, but you only got beer money." The same is true in life when you get out of your lane and live beyond your means; it is only a matter of time before you stand out, look stupid and get burned.

It reminds me of a teammate I had out in Oakland. He claimed to have a lavish house and Bentley, but I refused to believe it. "Man, you don't have a Bentley," I'd tell him. "If you had a Bentley, it'd be with you here in Oakland," I'd say. You don't buy a quarter-million-dollar car and leave it in another state for someone else to watch. He'd just keep saying, "Man, I got the car. I got the house."

I asked for pictures, but there were no pictures. I probably heckled him for about a year until one day I got a call from him, asking, "Hey Phil, Where you at?" I told him I was just leaving the practice facility. As I walked out, there was a Bentley parked out front. I heard the engine cut off and saw my teammate get out. "Told you I had a Bentley," he said. Here was a guy whose ego wouldn't let him admit to me he didn't really have a Bentley and million-dollar home. He went out and bought it just to shut me up. Now, maybe he could afford it, but most likely he got out of his lane and put on a show in order to get my stamp of approval. Now, when I look back at this story, I wonder whether he was telling the truth or just leased it to one-up me. The reality is less important than the fact: here was a guy who probably had a beer budget and champagne taste. He was probably just another football player living above his already considerable means.

I had another friend, a pro athlete, who lived his life in the fast lane. We decided to take a trip to Vegas and because it was a special occasion, he insisted that we take a private jet. I have no idea whether he had a time-share in the plane or just rented it for the weekend. Since it was probably a $20 million plane, there's no way he owned it (that's Tiger Woods money). But as we sat there, feet stretched out on the recliner, he looked over at me and said, "This is how we roll now. There's no other way."

I responded, "No, this is how *you* roll. I'm good with a window seat." Even on a private jet I was still trying to think of myself as retaining some sense of humility. My life was still flying commercial, despite the occasional Gulfstream VI lift.

Anyone can live beyond their means. Baseball player Curt Schilling blew $50 million, his entire fortune, developing video games. People who make seven figures need to stay in the seven-figure lane, not the eight-to-nine-figure lane. It requires a certain level of self-confidence and stability to acknowledge that the person riding next to you has a few more zeros at the end of their paycheck.

Guys and Girls Just Wanna Have Fun

Now, I'd like to welcome you to the world of what I call "Fun Friends." Please pay close attention to the following definition:

Fun Friend [fən frend] ▸ *n.*
1. On call at all times and down for anything.
2. Helps you spend money, not grow your money.
3. Viewed as the hired clown; whether you laugh at him or with him, there for entertainment purposes.
4. Synonymous with Hype People.
5. The devil on your shoulder that doesn't recognize limits.
6. If you're lucky, in rare cases a Fun Friend can also be a true friend.

When you enter this new world, there are plenty of Fun Friends that suddenly pop up around you during your downtime. Sometimes too many. Think back to the analogy of the shaking and rattling Pinto, versus the smooth riding Mercedes-Benz, driving on the freeway. With Fun Friends, the risk of steering the Pinto into the fast lane skyrockets. They're spending your money, and they're encouraging you to keep spending! You see the Benz and go, *that's where I want to be*. This kind of driving on cruise control can lead to a fast burnout. Before you know it, that Pinto's going to be smoking hot and you will be pulling off to the shoulder with your hood raised, waiting for roadside assistance. Better to drive that Pinto smoothly in your lane until you can afford an upgrade—maybe the Acura instead of the Mercedes.

Yes, life can be like cruising on a five-lane California freeway. The upgrades will come if you drive at the right speed, they'll just come a little slower. Sometimes slow is good. It gives you time to think and make the right moves.

More Finances, More Romances

I had a Fun Friend, a professional athlete, who entered the New Money world with me around the same time. He didn't know how to be alone, so he had a different woman with him at all times. He would fly in four to five women a week, no matter where he was. It was easy to pull off because he had two places in the same city. This is not uncommon in the world of NFL players coming into money. One time, one of my other homeboys flew in fifteen women for a party. He didn't care if they knew. It was no secret. He even got all the girls on the same party bus. I wouldn't be surprised if by the end of the night each lady had her time with my Fun Friend. You can approve of this or not—I'm not going to judge his behavior, especially if the women were willing. But that's just the way it was.

Know this: flying friends from here to there, men or women, gets expensive. I, too, paid for my fair share of flights, and paying for flights on a routine basis can drain anybody's pockets. Flights ran anywhere from $200 to $1,000, depending on how late I booked the flight. I pulled a few last-minute flights, and yes, they were incredibly expensive. The airlines know that if you want to get somewhere right away, you'll pay a pretty premium. I went through a phase of buying plane tickets for girls weekly—sometimes twice a week. Some were repeats but not regulars. If you fly them out on a steady basis, they start thinking you really have something going on. They'll also think you have more money than you really do. Why do so many of us succumb to this expensive habit? Well, once you fly a woman out, you've secured a good night. Part of the process of growing up with new money is thinking with the area above the neck and not below the waist. This shouldn't be difficult.

When I traveled to a big event, like an NBA All-Star Game weekend, I'd get five rooms—one for me, one for my homeboys, and two to three for different women that I could entertain throughout the weekend. I didn't have to worry about one girl finding out about the other because I could easily afford to take one girl on a date while I had the other girl back at the hotel. I could send one out shopping or to get a massage while I was having dinner with the other. You see, nothing was in singular form anymore. It wasn't just *a* new car, it was new *cars, plural.* It wasn't just *a* house, it was *houses.* It wasn't just a nice girlfriend, it was *ladies,* ladies, and ladies, in as big of a group as I could handle.

Is this an efficient way to think and conduct your social life? Probably not, but I'll leave that up to you. But this is what new money did to me. Remember, I had Superman Syndrome. My attitude was simple. I used a rap lyric to show me the way. Like that one line in Lil Wayne's song: "It ain't trickin' if you got it."

All of this abundance brought on competition. We weren't NFL players for nothing—we had a competitive streak like nobody's business. I hardly ever turned down a challenge. Sometimes, at a party, we'd start showcasing our ladies. The women would show up, and we would rate them. If it was a tie, then one of our homeboys voted for the tiebreaker. On occasion, we'd agree that we both had bad women. This is nothing to brag about, I admit. But this is how we rolled when we were immature and didn't know any better.

This behavior is not something I am proud of today, but as it was happening—all that money, all those good times, the power, the fun—it just felt too tempting to turn down. I don't know a single professional football player from my early days that didn't behave like this at some point. We were adults only in age, still acting like teenagers.

Fancy Cars and Stars to Late-Night Stripper Bars

It didn't stop with the girls—the competition and the fast-lane moves went beyond the ladies. It permeated every area of our lives.

I remember when a teammate from Miami and I flew out to L.A. to do a commercial shoot for Reebok; we were at our hotel waiting for our complimentary rental and saw Mike Ornstein, who worked for Reebok at the time, walking towards us in the lobby. "You want a Bentley?" he shouted. Hell yeah we want a Bentley. "You fucking guys," he said, smirking, "I just don't get it. We get guys like Marshall Faulk, Pro Bowlers, Hall of Famers, even your own cousin, Jevon Kearse, that are happy driving a Buick. You two motherfuckers from Miami come out here and you want to drive Bentleys." Long story short, we didn't get our Bentley, but we got a Benz. Mike and I still speak from time to time, and I know we can sit back and laugh at that exchange today. Mike knew what we were all about way before we understood ourselves.

A typical day for my crew of Fun Friends usually involved shopping, women, eating, women, video games, women, gambling, women, alcohol, women, the club, and then more women. I felt like I had a class schedule. First period was breakfast. Second period was PE, a friendly Madden or NCAA Final Four competition on the gaming console. Rough life.

After lunch, I would hit the mall. I was mallin' and ballin', shoppin' and bottle poppin'. Hit Footlocker, then head to Burberry. It wasn't out of the ordinary for me to spend between $4,000 and $6,000 in one day. Sometimes, I would spend an extra couple thousand if a few of my homeboys were with me. I was going to look fashionable, regardless of the price. I was about fashion and smashin'.

After my lavish shopping spree, I repeated second period until it was time for the club. At the club, we bought bottles because bottles brought women. We learned fast that cash begets ass. We called those ladies "bottle vultures." It was too easy. I was spending 'em and bending 'em. If I were rolling with some other Newborn Millionaires, I would get my own table just because I could. After hours of popping bottles and reining in women, we would head to the strip club to finish out the night. That was usually our wind-down.

I was driving the Pinto, figuratively speaking, believing that I could live this lifestyle forever. I was a regular fast-lane driver, set on cruise control. I would soon find out that wasn't the case.

In Miami, it was a toss-up whether we ended our night at Rol-Lexx or Coco's strip club. If my boys and I were looking for good food, we went to Rol-Lexx, and if we were looking for the baddest ladies, we went to Coco's. I would chill for a bit with them and then head home. But we didn't head home without making our grand exit. The grand exit involved tossing a couple hundred singles into the air, throwing up the deuces and watching it rain as we exited the club. And just like before . . . it was all just because I could.

Of course, sometimes throwing so much money around got out of hand. I mentioned before that there were very few competitions I would turn down. Competition was second nature to me, so when we saw someone else throwing money, it became a battle about who had more flow to throw. Pretty ridiculous way to enjoy yourself, I know.

I remember flying to Atlanta to hang out with some of my celebrity friends. Like most nights, it ended at a strip club. This night in particular, a group of guys called BMF came in with big black duffle bags of money. BMF was a local gang. Within an hour, about $100,000 in cash had been thrown. I remember them looking over in the direction of my buddies and throwing up their hands as if to say, "Where's your money at? You say you have money, let's see it." Throwing $10,000 to $20,000 was common, but I had never seen $100,000 thrown before. It rained harder that night in the strip club than a summer storm in South Florida.

That's when my Pinto started to shake, and I was reminded of the lane I belonged in. Thankfully, I was in my right mind that night and didn't step up to the challenge. I stayed in my lane, pulled out my umbrella, and watched as the BMF made it thunder.

Silly as it sounds, it was impressive, even thinking about it years later. Today, I now know the difference between BMF and me was that my income was getting taxed, theirs wasn't. I think it's easy for many NFL players that grew up in the hood to identify with drug dealers, which makes it even more difficult to recognize the risks you run by competing with them financially. At some point my money and resources could go flat or run out. Their money came in on a continuous stream. It only ran out if they got caught, or worse. They lived for the moment. They had no 401(k) plan. Their line of work required them to enjoy every moment because their next wasn't guaranteed.

At the end of the day, I recognized that although they lived for now, when they got caught they had no plan B. When my NFL career ends, I still have plans B through Z. I have plenty of options. Luckily, I eventually realized that strip clubs became a conflict of interest. The strippers and I have two things in common: we both enjoy sex and we both enjoy making money. Now, if I gave them money for sex, it's two points for the strippers (assuming they like their work), one point for Phillip. I lose. Mostly, I could have sex for free. I already bought the booty when I bought the bottles.

I probably spent more than a million dollars with women in strip clubs and nightclubs in a ten-year span. That's not an exaggeration. Was it worth it? I paid and got played. But trust me, the feminists who think I was exploiting the sisterhood should think again. They got the better end of the bargain. I was an official sponsor of the Girl Scouts; I paid for a lot of cookies.

Lesson well learned. Every lesson is a blessin'.

Back to My Lane, Cruising at a Reasonable Speed

Here is a story about humility, celebrity, and your own station in the economic order. There is no better place to find out where you stand than in Los Angeles. In L.A., no matter who you are, you will find someone who is more famous than you, richer than you, or better looking than you. The writer E. B. White once said that people go to New York City hoping to become lucky. I think you can say that people go to L.A. also hoping to get lucky, but if they don't, they can still dream. It is a city of dreams and dreamers.

I remember once I was in L.A., waiting for my homeboy Lonnie, who was late getting out of a studio music session, I got hungry and dipped into one of my favorite restaurants, Urth Caffé, in Hollywood. It's known for its coffee, but I like the food because it's organic and they have nice breakfast. As I was waiting for my order, my eyes were instantly drawn to a blonde woman in a white dress. She was drop-dead gorgeous, but in L.A. that in itself is not unusual. I watched as she smiled at her server. Man, her smile was beautiful. She looked familiar, but when you're in L.A., familiar could mean a famous actress, singer, or just someone you've seen on TV. It's almost impossible not to bump into a celebrity.

In any case, I noticed this girl, and, for a moment, she glanced my way. Our eyes locked. As I was about to mouth hello, my server set down my breakfast.

My waiter interrupted this reverie. "Do you need anything else, sir?" he asked. I made brief eye contact with him to say *No thank you*, but that was long enough for the mystery blonde to get back to the conversation with her friend.

I tried to pace my breakfast so I could leave at the same time she did, hoping to speak to her. To pass the time, I started talking to the guy next to me. He had a camera with a foot long telephoto lens. He was an older guy—late fifties, I guessed. He said he was a professional photographer (as if I couldn't tell). Every few seconds I diverted my eyes back to that beautiful smile to make sure she was still there. Mid-sentence, I noticed she got up. I was about to get up, too, but the cameraman beat me to it.

Then I noticed another half dozen other photographers around the restaurant. They all jumped after the girl and started shooting her as she walked across Main Street to her friend's car.

She was a somebody. That was the first time I had seen the paparazzi in full force in a public venue; I can still see the flash and hear the clicks of the cameras. She got in an old-school car and the paparazzi continued snapping pictures.

When she drove away, the photographer who sat next to me said, "I thought you were Amber's bodyguard the way you kept looking over at her every few seconds."

I was stunned by his remark. I mean, sure, I was wearing all black, but her bodyguard? I thought, *Come on, I'm Phillip Buchanon, a pro football player.* That didn't seem to matter much there. She didn't know who I was because I wasn't a celebrity who was on TV often enough to be recognized. In la-la land, where celebrity sightings are commonplace, nobody in the restaurant recognized the model and actress Amber Heard. Or if they did, they were cool enough not to indicate that they noticed.

When I stood up and put my feet back on the ground, there wasn't a paparazzo in sight. That woman with the beautiful smile was gone, and I hadn't even been able to say hello. Amber disappeared, but her trail put me back into my lane.

Chapter 3

From Family Cookouts . . .
to Handouts . . . to Fallouts

When You Tell Them No, They Talk About You

Do I believe people were genuinely happy for me when I made it? Yes, certainly. Do I believe that more people were happy at the potential benefits for them? Yes, also true. But there is a big difference. The majority of people that I knew believed they were supposed to be living like I was. They were under the false assumption that I would support them forever. Sadly, very few people had my best interest in mind, and those that did were genuinely happy to see another kid make it out of the hood. The rest were a very sad lot, especially as I look back over the past decade. I decided to call them "Adult Abusers."

Adult Abusers [ə-dəlt ə-byüzərz] ▶ *n.*
1. Influential adults in a person's life that manipulate or exploit the person who has recently come into money.
2. See a person who has recently come into money as a form of life support; cutting off their money is like turning off their oxygen.
3. Of, or pertaining to, childhood friends, parents, grandparent, aunts, uncles or other family members. This is only a partial list.

First, they start with seemingly altruistic motives. They get involved in your financial life with the reasoning that they're going to protect you from all those outside predators in the business world.

They're going to look out for *your* money. In my experience, at the end of the day, all of them thought they could manage my money better than I could. This kind of logic was incredibly misguided because they had no experience with this amount of wealth. Some of them could barely manage their grocery budgets.

The voices of my grandmother and mother echoed in my head: "You need to let me run your money." Or, "You don't know what you're doing. I can manage your money better than you." The truth is right in your face: nobody will take care of your money like you will. Nobody will care about your financial well-being because they will not be looking at it from your point of view. You will make mistakes, sometimes a lot of them, but the goal is to minimize and learn from them.

We Made It Now

The Adult Abusers in my life were varied, but the majority were among family and some close friends. A few of my friends and relatives expected to have what I had: the same cars, houses, wardrobe, and jewelry. It was as if I bought the winning lotto ticket and everyone had agreed to split my winnings but me. The financial position I was in was not a result of pure luck. Many years of hard work, dedication, ability, and some luck gave me my worth. It wasn't fair for everyone to jump on the bandwagon I'd built; it was bound to crumble under all that weight. When I thought about it, I remembered not the generosity I was expected to show, but all the workouts, practices, and sweaty mornings running through the neighborhood, exhausted before breakfast. Were they there for that?

I've always wanted to give back and do nice things for others, especially for family, but there's a difference between doing stuff for people that need the money and doing stuff for people who abuse your money. I have always deeply believed that I had an obligation to help my family. When I was young I was told, "When you're blessed, you're supposed to share those blessings." Most right-minded people have this feeling. In retrospect, I think that my belief evolved into knowing the difference between sharing my blessings with my family in times of *need* and not in times of *want*. I just couldn't meet their every desire, and I didn't feel it was my role to do so.

At first, it was hard to recognize the difference between need and want. You must learn the difference, or you will end up depressed, crazy, broke, or all three. If you remember nothing else from this book, remember that. I felt trapped in a cycle by my family. *Give me this. Give me that.* It didn't matter how much money I gave them, it never seemed to be enough. Shelly Finkel, a former boxing manager and promoter, summed it up well: "People you have known all your life can't function without you."

It took other people pointing out the adult abuse for me to realize that my family was strangling me financially. Once a woman friend of mine tried to set me straight. She told me, "I've known you for a while now, Phil, and I admire what you're doing for your family. But if you keep on doing all this stuff, you will probably be broke." Point taken. But then she went on, "I hear them talking when you're not around about the things you supposedly owe them." In reality, I owed most of them nothing.

It eventually hit me then that I was getting conned. Why did a bystander observing my situation see the potential for it to get ugly before I did? It was in that moment that I woke up. I began to assess and reform my spending patterns. It was at that moment that I realized that if I remained reckless, I would end up checkless.

Financial Wealth versus My Mental Health

Who do you blame when you veer off the tracks? It's never just one person, in my view. My biggest disappointment was my immediate family, but when you take a long look in the mirror, it's yourself. You allow everything to happen.

I thought I knew better than to fall for tricks, but I allowed myself to get sidetracked. With my biggest disappointment came the hardest lesson. I needed to take a step back from my family in order to preserve my wealth and not to end up another statistic.

I went into isolation. Some may call this cowardly, but it takes courage. I was lost in my thoughts, alone most of the time and locked into a zone of self-assessment—reviewing my life and thinking about an alternative future.

During this time, I felt the most conflicted. I grew up thinking that when I had money, I would take care of my family, but I never thought they would be ungrateful. There were certain situations that I needed to take myself out of. Many phone calls were stressful, and the worst were from my mother and grandmother. You cannot believe some of the abuse I took. Let me offer a few examples.

When things got tense, my grandmother would say, "Phillip, don't you dare hang up the phone. I'm not hanging up until you agree to give me money." Another conversation I had with my mom around Valentine's Day comes to mind. She said, "If it isn't money, don't send it. Fuck the cards and candy. If it ain't fucking money, don't send that shit." Can you imagine hearing those words from your mother?

Would I cuss them out or would I hang up on them? To me, both options were equally disrespectful. I'm not a disrespectful person, never was. To avoid either, I stopped taking their calls. If anything, I spoke to them through someone else. Ultimately, I removed myself from them. For too long, I went along with their demands, and I finally reached a point where I needed to step away in order to gain a better perspective. I was frozen in a state of confusion. I wanted to go back to simple problems, like not having enough of my grandma's homemade cornbread at dinner.

But it wasn't about grandma's cornbread anymore; now it was about grandma trying to get *my* bread.

From Family Cheers to Silent Tears

After several years in the NFL, I began to change how I looked at things. I didn't exactly give up my party lifestyle completely, but I began spending a lot of late nights by myself trying to figure things out. I often questioned why I was in this position, but I was faithful to the idea that if I were going to have problems, I would rather have problems with money. The really strange thing about this phenomenon is this: when you have a lot of money and it's going out of your account faster than you can imagine, you automatically think that it will stop once you start making more money. And in my career, more money did come in. But the problems just multiplied.

What sounds better? More money, more problems, or no money, more problems? Bob Dylan has a great line in one of his songs: "When you got nothin', you got nothin' to lose." Well, being poor stinks for anyone, but daily living is quite simple, isn't it? It's just getting to the next meal, the next place to sleep, and the next day. There's nothing heroic in being poor. It's just uncomplicated.

Would I go back to having my family the way it once was before I had money? No. I'm a go-getter. I never wanted to live paycheck to paycheck. Perhaps this is why I felt so conflicted. Some may argue that it boils down to values: money versus family. But I think it's more complicated than that; it's about balancing both. It's not a matter of choosing one over the other. Looking back, I would have done things differently, but there would have been family dilemmas to deal with no matter what. Still, it was hard and it was depressing at times. I even broke down and shed a few tears. Most often the crying came late at night, sitting on my balcony, where not even the brightest star could light up the darkness surrounding my thoughts. You want it all to go away, but it's not that simple. You wake up in the morning, and if you haven't done anything to make substantive changes in your life, it's the same old story.

If Not Family, Whom Can You Trust?

Sometimes it was the people closest to me that did the most hurtful things. In order to understand the complexities of my relationships with my family, I need to tell you the story of Uncle Two-Face. I'm using a pseudonym because he will undoubtedly read this, and I don't want to cause any more discomfort and embarrassment to him or those who disappointed me. Uncle Two-Face had two personas: the good uncle and the bad one. I always knew from a young age that my uncle had some character flaws. We all have them. But I didn't see the other side until I had a large bank balance.

Uncle Two-Face broke my heart. He was as close to a surrogate father figure as I could hope for after my Uncle Curtis died. He was the youngest of my uncles and was only about five years older than me. He was the first person to take me in the backyard and put me through drills back in my Pop Warner days. He gave the best run-through-the-wall speeches. He was the personification of motivation. He knew how to give a pep talk to a young boy with dreams and ambition. Literally, he'd make you want to run through a wall for him.

When I became a New Money Millionaire, those speeches turned into talks that felt more like exploitation than friendly family chats, talks that were more about running through my money than anything else. I also caught wind that he was telling women around Ft. Myers that he had a $300,000 credit line coming to him. The implication was, if these ladies were smart, they would join his team. My weakness was that I saw enough of my Uncle Curtis in those inspirational speeches that I never turned my back on him.

Of course, I did give Uncle Two-Face some money. But after months of pressing me for more, I had a huge altercation with him. He was not satisfied. $5,000 here or $10,000 there was not enough for him. However, he had no idea how many people were asking me for money. Even if he did, I'm not sure he would have cared.

He called me and it was a phone conversation I will never forget. After the usual pleasantries, he asked me for money. I told him I wasn't going to give him any more. He blurted out, "You wipe your ass with $10,000 on any given night, so why you making a big deal about giving me money?" I kept my composure, and I just kept telling him that I was turning off the spigot. No more money.

What he said next stung like salt in a fresh cut: "If I ever see you back at the crib, I'm going to rob your ass." This was some way to end a phone call to your nephew who was never anything but generous. I was thinking the following: *Don't try to act like you're from the street when I really know your résumé.* But I didn't say it. As confident as I was that he wouldn't go through with his threat, I knew better than to test him.

This situation with Uncle Two-Face put a strain on the relationship I had with other family members. Simply put, I didn't want to spend time with other family members because Uncle Two-Face might show up at anytime starting drama.

Uncle Two-Face told everybody in my immediate family that I wasn't doing enough for everyone else. So they began to believe Uncle Two-Face and not trust me. So, simply put, I didn't want to spend time with any of them. In the end, Two-Face was just another Adult Abuser.

It's an awful story, isn't it? But read on, it gets worse. There were people closer to me than my uncle who were also serial Adult Abusers.

In God We Trust . . . Not Grandma

I often prayed to God for guidance when I couldn't depend on my immediate family for it, but I got to the point where even my own faith was tested. My family would use God to get money. The following stories about my grandmother are true, and they're both pathetic and funny—closer to which, I'm not sure. I'll let you be the judge.

My grandma would start, "You know the saying 'In God We Trust'? That's God's money."

"Grandma, it's my name on the bank account, not God's," I'd say.

"Pull out your money, let me show you something," she'd say. So I'd go in my wallet and pull out a dollar bill.

"You don't have any hundreds in there?"

"Yeah, I've got one right here," I'd respond, pulling out a Benjamin.

Then she would take that hundred, point to the wording, and read it aloud: "In God We Trust." Without hesitating, she would put the bill directly in her pocket. The first time she did this, I gave her an astonished look. She gave me a look back, like who was I to even question her?

"What? I need to go get some more tobacco," she said. If it wasn't tobacco she needed money for, it was to bet at the dog track. I had a hunch she was gambling away a lot of the money I gave her.

"But Grandma, that's God's money."

She'd say, "Boy, God would want you to give me some money, so that's what you should do."

This also reminds me of the time she told me she needed a Bentley. I said, "For what?"

"To drive to church," she said.

I fell for the pull-out-your-money trick a few times until I wised up and adjusted my donations. I wouldn't take out anything bigger than a twenty-dollar bill. I even started putting the dollar bills on top because she'd damn near pat me down when I'd walk in the house. "Whatcha got in there? You remember that saying, now. That's God's money . . ." she'd say as she felt for my wallet.

If that's true, then I am almost certain my mother got a direct call from God telling her to hold all of my money. Soon after the draft, she told me that I owed her a million dollars for raising me for the past eighteen years. Well, that was news to me. If my mother taught me anything, it's that this is the most desperate demand that a parent can make on a child. The covenant of having a child is simply that you give your child everything possible, and they owe you nothing beyond a normal amount of love and respect. There is no financial arrangement. If you get old and infirm, and your kids are around to help you out at that point, then you're lucky. It's not written in the social contract. The mothers and fathers of the world have been rearing their kids for generations—in every culture imaginable—and it's a one-way street when it comes to money. If they pay you back someday, and you really are going through hard times, then that's just a bonus, a gratuity for being a great mother or father.

My mother had said my debt to her was a million dollars before, but this time she was more serious than ever. If you do the math, one million dollars divided by eighteen years of raising me was approximately $55,555.55 a year in restitution. Except, at age seventeen I decided to move out of my mom's house, choosing to live with a close friend and his father because I no longer felt secure in my own home. Why, you ask? Because my mother let people come in and out of our house and take what they wanted. So technically, even if we went by her logic, I only owed her $944,444.44 for her services over seventeen years.

Is it petty that I'm knocking a year off her calculation? The fact that I have written this paragraph enrages me, merely because I'm entertaining the thought that her argument had any logic at all. Maybe if I had become super rich, I could have written the check and been done with it. But, like blackmail, there is never any end, is there?

Please do not think I'm being ungrateful or cheap. I had already followed the unwritten rule of any NFL New Money Millionaire: I bought my mother a house. I also advised her to sell the old one I grew up in when I put a new roof over her head, but my mother had other plans. Instead of selling my childhood home, she decided to rent it to my aunt. So I had to finance my mother, the budding landlord. Only this wasn't an investment. It was an encumbrance, because I didn't share in my mother's profit-making scheme. For the next seven years, I continued to make mortgage and maintenance payments on *both* homes.

I learned from this expensive lesson that big-ticket purchases for family members, such as houses and cars, should be evaluated with the following questions in mind: If you were unable to make payments for these purchases, would that particular family member be able to make the payments? Twenty years from now, who will be paying the upkeep on the house? You or your family member?

Then there's the respect part of the equation. Are these family members respecting the gifts you give? For years, my mother left the lights on in the house without a thought as to how much I paid for electricity. This is a corollary of an old cliché that I've heard many times, that your kids won't turn out the lights when leaving a room until they grow up and have to pay their own utility bills. It used to refer to kids, but in my case it fit right in as applicable to my family of Adult Abusers.

Anger built up inside me as my mother collected rent from our old house and never offered a cent to offset the expenses. It got to a point that I had to kick her boyfriend out. She accused me of messing up her life. What she didn't see was that her boyfriend was pimping her and me out. He wasn't bringing anything to the table, just taking.

When I told my mother she would have to take care of the main-tenance after I paid off the mortgage on her house, she told me she would not be able to afford the upkeep on a house that big. In fact, she made it seem like it was my fault for picking out a house that big. In part, she was right. I bought her a house with my luxury taste and no real wisdom behind it. It was an uneducated purchase. Many NFL players choose a wiser route: they buy a reasonably sized home, pay for it in cash, keep it in their name, but gift it to their mother.

I tried giving my mother that option the second time around. I offered to buy her a comfortable house in my name for her to live in. This way she wouldn't have to take out any loans or put my little sister and brothers in a situation where the roof over their heads could be taken away. She'd move out of the house that was too big for her and into this new one. Instead, she opted for $15,000 cash. She told me that if the new house didn't have space for two living room sets, she didn't want it.

Here's what she really meant: she did not want to be embarrassed by downsizing from the home I'd originally bought for her. She was stubborn (a trait I get from her) and decided to take the cash despite my advice. I told her that if I gave her the $15,000, not to come calling when she got into trouble. Needless to say, she ended up calling. And, what's worse, she lost the house.

I found it ironic that my mother thought she could manage my finances better than I could, yet she could not provide proof of making any money from the schemes she had set up. One day I let my anger get the better of me and asked her, "If you're so smart, why haven't you put together a plan to make money off of the money that you are saving from the expenses you aren't paying?" The year I became a New Money Millionaire, I took every expense off of her hands except for food and fun money. This led her to challenge me to a money-making contest. "Oh, so you think you Phillip fucking Buchanon? Since you think you're smarter than your mother, we're going to have a competition," she said. "You give me a certain amount of money and you budget yourself a certain amount, and we will see who makes the most money from it." I laughed, giving her credit for another attempt (a creative one at that), but she tried to fool me again. She even played upon my weaknesses because she knew that I rarely turned down a competition. Of course, I never went for this little scheme because I knew there was no way I could win. My mother would never win either because she'd simply go through the cash in a hurry. Then she'd need another clever idea to get another check. I wasn't going to make the same mistake again.

I eventually learned how to deal with the numerous "family emergencies." Early on, I found myself in too many situations where some relative would come to me and claim they needed something fixed. So I'd write them a check; of course, the problem never got fixed. The check, however, always got cashed. By trying to fix a problem, I created an additional one for myself.

I finally learned how to cope with this type of request. I paid the bills directly to the company or handyman doing the work. It was amazing to see how my family responded when I told them I would take care of it. They tried to lay the heaviest guilt number on me. I can still hear their muttering tones with tinges of disgust: "Nah, man, I'm cool. Forget about it." This response meant they knew I was on to what they were up to. I had caught them red-handed, committing an act of adult abuse.

It took hundreds of thousands of dollars, far more than the cost of an Ivy League education, to learn this lesson. I can at least attribute it to my mother. It's true; mothers have a way of making you learn the most important lessons in life.

Spending Like There's No Tomorrow . . . May Ultimately Lead to Grief and Sorrow

If I lived every year like I did my first year as a New Money Millionaire, I'd be in serious debt. Perhaps I could have lived several more years, just breaking even. But I wanted to make my money grow; I wanted to preserve capital. For this, I had to reform my spending and saving habits, big time. I was ready to do that.

My flagrant spending and disregard for a dollar went unchecked for four years after I signed my first NFL contract. My stint with Houston almost ended my career without leaving me any new opportunities.

I received a healthy dose of reality: a combination of injuries and the sudden feeling that I was not going to fit in with the team's defensive philosophy. As a cornerback, I saw right away that I was going to hate playing football for the Texans.

The grass is not always greener on a new playing surface in another city. During my time in Houston, everything I did was crushed. The Texans' coaches wanted me to play how I played at Miami, but that made no sense. The plays we ran at Miami were not being called. I loved the city of Houston, and I thought being on a young team with an old college teammate, Andre Johnson, would be a good situation.

But what a mistake this decision was. The timing was bad because I was hoping to get a big contract. This was sort of a wake-up call. Being depressed about my career led to long nights of drinking and wishing this was all just a bad dream.

I kept reminding myself that I had a good attitude, I wasn't a bad guy, and I was certainly a hard worker—on the practice field and in the games. I gave it my all. I felt that most of my teammates were the same. Hard work was not the problem. The problem was that our team chemistry didn't allow us to work smart. We didn't put players in the right situations. We never talked about our issues to find common ground to make things work.

Our team's problems were just the beginning. They were compounded by injuries, and mine were no exception. The Texans mandated my rehab routine, and it was destined to fail. I would get up at 6:00 AM and get treatment at 7:00. I had to stay between the locker room and the treatment room. I hated this schedule because I couldn't be around my teammates. I would get treatment again at 11:00 AM or noon and I'd be sent home while my teammates were going to practice. This did nothing for my morale. The coaches had me come into the facilities for treatment only. I was told I couldn't attend meetings or practices until I was healthy enough to play. But this was during the actual season, and not being involved meant I would be left behind when it came to strategy and play design.

I knew I was a dead man walking. They did a great job at making me feel worthless. It was funny at times, but my teammates started calling me the "outlaw" or saying "You're a cancer"—mostly just to tease me because hanging around me at that time was bad news.

Eventually, low morale wafted its way through the entire locker room. It was so bad in Houston that either the coaches or management had people checking on players to see if they were out clubbing at night. If they found out about it, they would let you know. They'd tell us we couldn't go to certain nightclubs because they made it seem like Mafia or drug dealers were behind them. These nightclubs were not considered bad clubs, but this was their way of giving players a hard time after poor performances on the field.

Every NFL team has its own method of enforcing discipline and inspiring their players. But it's not like we were college students. You can't treat adults like little children and then expect them to act like adults.

So then it occurred to me that I had to start thinking smarter by opening up my mind to life after football. I was also blowing through a lot of money trying to find answers. All I found were fewer zeros in my account. I remember looking at my statement, and I was down to my last $400,000. I was no longer a millionaire.

In fact, I was a lot worse off than I thought. I had a negative net worth.

I had three home loans where I owed much more than $800,000. If those loans defaulted at the time, I would not only have been flat broke, but I'd have been facing bankruptcy. I would have been worse off than I was when I first came into the league, only now with a lot of big spender stories to tell. For the first few years I was only paying interest on those loans. An interest-only loan gives you the flexibility and freedom of lower monthly payments, but if you continue like that, you will never pay off what the loan is actually for (in my case, houses). This was a financial instrument used heavily during the housing boom whereby mortgage brokers and lenders told borrowers not to worry, their house values would continue to rise and they would cash out when they sold their homes.

The fact that I owned three houses sounds appealing. But, as I've said before, I didn't really own them. A house is not a real business investment unless you are renting it to someone else and making money within the first couple of months.

*   *   *

The life lesson I learned in Houston was an enduring one. Pro teams sign you because they have a specific use for your skills and talents. As soon as you don't fit with their program, they will do whatever it takes to make you feel unwanted or uncomfortable. And when the winds of discomfort begin to blow, you worry about your next job and your next paycheck.

Herman Edwards said this about professional football in *30 for 30: Broke*: "It's an opportunity. It's not a career . . . you don't know when your career's gonna end." By definition, an opportunity is merely a chance or a set of circumstances that make it possible for you to do something. For a professional football player, getting drafted is your chance. You have talent and there's a team out there that needs you. You're in the right place at the right time, and you're ready. The team needs you and you need them—those are the circumstances that make your window of opportunity possible. But just as quickly as that opportunity is given, it can be taken away. If only for this reason alone, it's a good idea to consider a signing bonus or even a first contract as nothing more than Head-Start Money.

Head-Start Money [hed-start mәnē] ▶ *n.*

1. Known as "turnkey money"; will start the engine but won't keep the engine running without appropriate maintenance.
2. A windfall that involves money that has a foreseeable end.
3. Money possibly obtained through lottery, inheritance, or professional contract.

A professional athlete's tenure in the league represents an opportunity with a finite duration; money you get up front should be Head-Start Money because you can't be a baller forever.

Learn to use Head-Start Money intelligently, or you will suffer the consequences. Like Charles Barkley once famously said in a TV commercial, "I am not a role model," at least not for the way I originally reacted to having sudden money thrown at me.

There are people that spend as much as they make. That's not a good position to be in; there's no wiggle room, no safety net. Worse still, there are people that spend *more* than they make. It's tempting in this great country of ours where credit abounds. So if you want to live life lavishly, go ahead. Just know that as soon as there's a negative in your bank account, the public (especially creditors) will have something to say about it.

However, if you're in the business of growing and saving money, you have to put a system of checks and balances into play and spend less than you earn. You need an alert on your smart phone. You have to budget, especially in the area of recreational spending. My best advice is to have a game plan before stepping foot in the club (or the hotel hot tub). Withdraw the amount of cash you plan to spend for the night earlier that day and leave your debit or credit card home. Have a cash-spending limit on that vacation with your friends. This takes the temptation out of the equation and assures you remain in control. Once the cash is gone, it's time to leave, either the club or Anguilla. And if you're real smart, you may even consider leaving *before* it's gone.

If you're a competitor, use it to your advantage. Don't be like me that first year as a New Money Millionaire. It's not about who can make it rain the hardest, who has the most cars, or who spent the most money. Start competing to be on top financially—be the one who saved the most, the one who has more assets than liabilities, the one who has identified the best mentor. You're never going to have as much money as Warren Buffet or Bill Gates, so why worry about keeping that kind of score? They didn't, and you shouldn't. The reason they kept their vast fortunes is that they learned not only how to invest but how to manage their money. Ultimately, aim to be remembered for the success you obtain beyond your Head-Start Money.

Don't Go Through Life, Grow Through Life

That's a quote that I live by, from Eric Butterworth, the Canadian author and educator. I've now confronted all of the problems associated with my profession: injuries, money issues, family, and getting traded to new teams. Watch those who are in faster lanes than yours, and let them inspire you, but don't feel like you have to jump into their lane right away. Know that everyone's path is different—full of various bumps and curves. Draw inspiration from others, but know that you must also follow your own route. It's not about reinventing the wheel; it's about picking the right set of tires for your ride. And remember, you're in a Pinto, not a Bentley or even a Benz. It is about individual hard work and discipline.

Find a successful person you admire and look to model and revise their methods to fit your life. If you don't know who that person is yet, engage in conversation with others. Seek them out. I always make time to talk with new people, even if it's brief. You can walk away with at least one important thing from any conversation you have. Try observing; take notice of the little details. When having a conversation, listen more and talk less; listen 80 percent of the time and talk 20 percent. By listening a lot, you learn a lot. Even if you don't learn anything, you will have an important takeaway. The point of any conversation with someone new is to get to know the other person.

Once you find the person that inspires you to change lanes, model their way, but make it your own. There is a fine line between modeling someone's plan and copying. When you copy, you are cheating. A person who cheats on a test may have an A imprinted on his or her transcript, but it's an empty A. If you cheat, you lack real experience and knowledge. You've cheated yourself and not just the system. In the end, life is simply an open-book test.

Without new knowledge there is no new growth. Too often we seek a shortcut but find ourselves facing a dead end. You don't want a dead end, you want to be able to look back in the rearview mirror and see how far you've come. You want options to get to your destination. Acknowledge that the temptation to cheat can be eliminated by asking for help. Get help and be grateful. Let your dreams fuel your tank. Own your lane. Excel to accelerate. Unfortunately, most of the accelerating I did my first few years in the league got me a lot of cool memories but depleted my bank account faster than I ever could have realized.

CHAPTER 4

Getting Jacked While Giving Back

It wasn't just my family that changed—it was everyone around me. People who had always been close got closer, and people who had just been acquaintances before were suddenly claiming stronger ties. I can't tell you how many times I heard, "*We* made it now, Phil." I winced. *What do you mean we?* I thought. There were people who genuinely wanted to help, but there were also Adult Abusers around every corner. And then there were the friends I thought I could trust and had known since childhood who turned out to be rotten. Joe Nocera, writer and *New York Times* columnist, once said, "Guys you trust shouldn't be corrupt."

Unfortunately, I had many a run-in with Historical Friends who I thought I could rely on, but who turned out to be totally unprincipled.

Historical Friend [his-tô-rik(ə)l frend] *n.*
1. Met early in life, usually before age seventeen.
2. Commonly referred to me as "dawg," "cousin," "brotha from anotha," etc.
3. Often met through extracurricular activities (Pop Warner football or Little League, clubhouse for the neighborhood kids, the local convenience store, etc.)
4. Potential to evolve into a true friend, though highly unlikely.
5. After age seventeen, meetings and conversations become more sporadic and less spontaneous.

Let Your Guard Down and Risk Getting Put Underground

Probably the most memorable incident with a sketchy Historical Friend happened at my home in Lithonia, a suburb of Atlanta, on the night of March 12, 2006. I was relaxing at my house with my longtime high school buddy, Nigel, when we heard a car door shut in the front yard.

It was 3:00 AM, and I wondered who it could be.

It's a night I'll never forget. We'd just had an old friend over—we called him J.B.—but it was getting late and he had left a short while ago. We weren't expecting anyone else, so I was curious to see who it could be. Maybe J.B. had forgotten something. I was standing at my kitchen island, and I walked to the front door. I caught sight of five guys wearing all black through the door window. Then the front door slammed open. "Police, police! Get on the ground!" one of the guys shouted.

Police? What the hell was going on? My first reaction was that it was a sophisticated practical joke. *Somebody must be playing around with me,* I thought. Until I saw the guys come straight in and hit my homeboy. They flashed guns. That's when I realized I better get on the floor, because these guys weren't kidding around.

I lay down on the kitchen floor on my stomach, my eyes circling the room like two frantic searchlights. Two of the guys were pacing the kitchen—back and forth, back and forth—wired and antsy. The other three were walking through my 5,000-square-foot home; I heard their footsteps going up the stairs. Then I heard things falling to the ground and shattering. I tried to figure out which room it was they were ripping apart when one of the intruders smacked the back of my head with the handle of his gun. Blood started dripping into my eyes, down my cheek, and onto a puddle on the ground. I hadn't done anything to provoke it; this was his way of sending me a serious message that it was going to get worse if I didn't cooperate.

"Man, if you don't give me twenty thousand tonight, y'all going to die!" said the guy who had just smacked me in the back of the head. He was small and skinny, maybe 5'6", 150 pounds max, but talking like he owned the world, like he was tough. Before I could respond, he hit me again. I should have been worried about what was going on, but as he was hitting me in the head, demanding money in a voice too big for his body, all I kept thinking was that if he didn't have a gun I'd mop the floor with his ass.

"Where is that tall-ass nigga? Is he coming back?" he yelled.

J.B.? He was certainly taller than either Nigel or me. Were they standing out there waiting for J.B. to leave? Was he still on the premises? If so, then he had set me up. A million thoughts were going through my head. I knew for sure this was a setup. They didn't just randomly pick my home.

I just didn't know if it was J.B. or Mo-Flo who had helped plan this. J.B. was one of the top all-around athletes during my era. I was sure he'd be headed to a pro football career until a freak nerve injury ended his hopes. Mo-Flo was another Historical Friend I'd grown up with; I started my football career with him. We played on the Riverdale Wildcats Pop Warner team together and later for our Lehigh high school team. Mo-Flo's career was derailed when he was thrown off the University of Mississippi team for violating team policy.

From the jump, everything between Mo-Flo and me was always about competition—from girls to who was better dressed to who was the fastest or scored the most touchdowns. Mo-Flo claimed that if it weren't for him I never would have made it as a pro football player.

Once, Mo-Flo was in a tight jam in California, so Nigel and a couple of my relatives talked me into helping him out for a couple of months until he got a job. Of course that didn't happen, and before I knew it the four months had turned into about two years. I had just recently kicked him out for good when I found out he forged my signature and cashed a $5,000 check that I had gotten from the

NFL 401(k) plan. Which is why I thought Mo-Flo may have set me up. If he did, he probably was getting a piece of the haul. He may have needed the money more than J.B. But, then again, Mo-Flo and J.B. had been hanging out recently, so it certainly was possible they were in this together.

Laying on my kitchen floor, I honestly thought J.B. or Mo-Flo might even have actually been in the house, out of my sight, telling the thieves where everything valuable was located. But the truth was, I wasn't really sure who was behind this, and I wanted the guys in my kitchen to know who I was. I wanted them to know what they were getting into because we were not street thugs.

If they were going to do something stupid, like kill me, they needed to know that it was going to be a big deal. There would be serious consequences for killing me. So when the guy who clocked me on the head stopped for a minute to talk to one of his crew, I had my chance. Letting these thugs know I had acclaim, name and NFL fame probably saved my life.

"My name is Phillip Buchanon," I told them. "I played football at the University of Miami. I was a first-round draft pick for the Oakland Raiders." This turned out not to be such a great idea.

"Oh, so you're a superstar," replied the skinny guy. "Okay, superstar, if you don't give me twenty thousand in cash tonight, I'm going to kill y'all." Then he went over to Nigel, who lay on the other side of the kitchen island. He continued taking his aggression out on Nigel. Nigel wasn't taking it well; he wasn't staying calm and going with the flow. Instead, he was rolling and cursing at the skinny guy with the gun like he was going to get into it with him. I tried to give Nigel a look that told him to just chill. Didn't he realize that the guy with the gun makes the rules? Eventually the skinny guy left and was replaced by a bigger guy who just stood there making sure we didn't do anything crazy.

There was a pocket of peace for about twenty to twenty-five very long minutes. With the big guy overseeing us, we didn't dare

move or make a sound, but we could still hear the other guys running up and down the stairs in the background, going from the
basement and carrying all my stuff out through the garage. Nigel
and I just lay there, bruised and bleeding, with no easy escape and
no weapons to defend us. After a little while, the skinny guy came
back into the kitchen.

"Superstar, if you don't give me twenty thousand cash tonight,
right now, I'm going to kill your friend, and then I'm going to kill
you," he said.

I saw that Nigel was about ready to explode on this guy, so I
tried to balance the mood out and stay even-keeled. I said to the guy,
"Look, y'all can take everything in this house—the car, my wallet,
whatever you want just so you can get up out the house!"

At which point, Skinny walked over to me as he played with
his gun and told me to open my mouth. "Give me the money or I
will blow your fucking brains out," he said, sticking the gun in my
mouth. This took my mind off the guys in skullies wheeling out my
sixty-inch flat-screen, my clothes, all my valuables. The gun in my
mouth put the focus on staying alive.

"Superstar, where is the money?" yelled Skinny, when another
one of the guys who I hadn't seen yet came in.

"Man, just chill. Just chill," said the new guy.

"I am chill," said Skinny. Then he pointed to Nigel and me and
told us to stand up. "Stand up and strip," he said. Outside, I could
hear the door to my old-school 1973 Impala open and close, so I
figured that was their U-Haul.

I started taking off my bloody T-shirt, and Skinny screamed at
me to take off my diamond earrings and turn them over. As I took
them off, the other guy yelled at me to hurry. I was boiling with anger, but I was wise enough to know not to do anything stupid. So I
handed him the earrings and continued to take off my boxers, shorts,
socks, and shoes.

"Hold hands and walk upstairs," he commanded Nigel and me.

As Nigel and I went upstairs, completely naked, there was an ee-rie silence all around us; the only thing we heard was the wood floors creaking with each step. When we got to the second floor, Skinny ordered us to lie in the hallway between the two guest bedrooms. The next thing I knew, the sheets from the linen closet were being thrown on top of us.

"Don't talk. Don't move. Or you'll lose your life fucking around with me."

It was like he was planning an execution-style murder, buck na-ked, with sheets over our heads. I placed my hands over my head thinking that it might at least slow down the penetration of a bullet to the head. I know, I know. That's a very weird, very stupid thought. But when you're under this kind of stress and someone has stuck a gun in your mouth, you think about weird, stupid things because all you're hoping for is to stay alive. I forced myself to think that this wouldn't be the end of me. I culled all the faith I had within me and I prayed for my life, for Nigel and me to come out of this okay.

Nigel, meanwhile, lay there muttering to himself, "I wish I had my gun. They caught us off guard. I wish I had my gun." Nigel had misplaced his priorities. First you worry about survival, then you plot your revenge.

Time started to slow down under the sheets, in the dark, and I just kept replaying the last ninety minutes in my head, picturing the faces of my invaders, hearing their voices. I began thinking again about who had set me up. How could I have let myself get blindsid-ed? What would happen if I died? I wondered what my family would think. They might assume I was set up or that it had something to do with a female or a relationship gone bad. Or they might think that I was just hanging around the wrong guys.

And that's when it hit me—that's the one thing they would get right. I was hanging out with the wrong guys. It didn't matter who betrayed me. It just mattered that someone I knew thought nothing of planning a robbery like this.

Then I wondered what my fans would think about it. They would probably think it was just another tragic story of a talented guy who lived life on the edge, or another dumb athlete with too much money who got involved with the wrong kind of people. Or they would think that I was a really bad guy and managed to cover up my dark side. They would be partially right.

All these thoughts were rolling around in my head, bumping into each other, until I heard the sound of my car starting. I knew the distinct roar of my old Impala—light blue magic on 22" rims with a souped-up 502 engine. After Nigel and I heard it being driven away, we lay there for a couple of minutes just to be safe. Assuming they were gone, I got up and ran to my bedroom to get the gun that I kept next to my bed. It wasn't there. I walked out of my room, and Nigel was coming from the guest room where he'd kept his own weapon down the hall. His gun was gone, too. (Readers take note: the South has an active gun culture. Legal weapons possession is very common in Georgia and Florida. More people than you think own guns in the name of home protection. But since this incident, I realize that having a gun around can just make things worse. Guard gates and an alarm system make me feel more secure.)

We found clothes to wear, and we ran down the stairs looking in every direction because we still weren't sure if anyone was in the house. It was a mess. Clothes and shoes were scattered all over the floor. Next to a pair of my Adidas, there was a gun that didn't belong to Nigel or me. We crept out of the back door of the basement and ran up the hill to my next-door neighbor's house; they didn't answer their door. So we started knocking on doors and ringing the doorbells at other neighbors' houses until finally someone came to their door. "We've been robbed," Nigel said. That was an understatement. He asked them to call the police.

On our way back to my house, Nigel and I stopped and stood in the middle of the road, stunned in the still of the morning dark. By now, it was around 4:45 AM. I looked toward my house—all the lights were on and the front door and garage were wide open. You could see straight through into the dining room, and had a full view of the stairs. Nigel was still talking: "Man, what the fuck just happened? This shit is crazy." He was rambling on and on, saying, "I know Mo-Flo had something to do with this. I just wish I had my gun when we were in the kitchen. Just when you think everything is cool, someone flips the script. Well, that will never happen again on my watch."

All I could think about was J.B. leaving fifteen minutes before the guys came. All I wanted to know was who set me up. Whether it was J.B., Mo-Flo or both of them. I wanted to handle the situation myself. I forgot about my professional life and as I stood looking at my empty house; I just wanted revenge. *Damn,* I thought. It felt like a movie.

Tupac was right. Anybody can get killed at any moment if somebody really wants to get you.

The police finally showed up a half hour later and asked the typical questions. They wanted to know if we were okay, if we had sustained any injuries worse than my head banging, what the night's events were, how many guys were there, what was stolen, and whether we thought we knew who could be behind the robbery. I didn't feel like answering a damn thing.

I hadn't even done an inventory of what was stolen. I didn't really have to. The gunmen took almost everything of value. They stole all of my personal possessions and jewelry—my watches, chains, and earrings—as well as most of my shoes and clothing. I was shopping earlier that day and had bought $4,000 to $5,000 in merchandise, and they stole all of it. They took my cell phone, my wallet, all of the flat-screen TVs, my Infiniti QX56 truck, and the Impala.

Besides everything they thought was valuable, they took the most cherished thing from me—my peace of mind.

Of course, in the end, I realized it could have been worse. Nigel and I were still alive, and that's what mattered. Everything else could be replaced. When I think about how the circumstances would have changed if Nigel had his gun or if I had mine, I realize that it's best we didn't have them around. I cannot even fathom what the headlines would have looked like in the *Miami Herald* the next day.

If I had my pearl-handled, chrome .45 at arm's reach, the thought of not using it would never have occurred to me. And Nigel? Forget it. Compared with me, he was by definition trigger-happy. If we had fired a few shots at them, it might have made them back off, but it also could have ended with someone getting shot. In fact, somebody probably would have been killed.

Eventually the police identified the crew and the robbery made the local newspapers. I never even appeared at the police station or in court, which always seemed strange. We just got a phone call from the police saying everything was okay. We were informed that two of the men who'd been in my house were now in custody. I didn't even have to press charges. I learned later that two of them went to jail for other crimes, and two eventually were killed.

J.B. claimed he had nothing to do with what happened, and he continued working in his family's business. He continued to text me like everything was fine, but I never responded.

As for Mo-Flo and his family, they denied any involvement in the break-in, but I have heard otherwise from some of our friends. The streets talk. I didn't accuse him of anything, but I was suspicious. Eventually, Mo-Flo was convicted of robbery and murder and is currently serving a long sentence. Perhaps my suspicion was warranted.

Money corrupts people, even the people you thought you knew. Historical Friends aren't always your true friends. That day, I learned to choose my friends wisely; keeping it real with Historical Friends almost got me killed.

I Didn't Know My Dawgs (Mo-Flo and J.B.) Had Rabies

Having money made it really hard for me to see what was true around me, particularly when it had to do with friends and family. But on the night of the robbery, the old me died and the new me was born. From that day on, I looked at everything in my life differently.

A week after the break-in, while I was at football workouts, my house was struck by lightning. That sort of thing doesn't even happen in the movies. Talk about biblical—it had to be a sign . . . a sign to be grateful for my life and to start reevaluating my actions and decisions. I realized quickly what was important to me. Today, I'm very conscious about the people I hang around and trust.

The money I earn is for my inner circle, my charity, and me. You have to be careful about whom you keep close in that inner circle. Tasting the metal of that chrome barrel in my mouth was like hitting a reset button. I'd let my guard down and almost got put underground. That night I wasn't just robbed by a group of thugs; my friends took me down. *With friends like these, who needs enemies?* I thought. The reason I've told you this story is simple: when you have any kind of notoriety, any kind of fame, and the money that accompanies it, you are immediately a target for something like this to happen. Let it be a cautionary tale. If you become a New Money Millionaire, your physical vulnerability increases dramatically . . . especially if you're a pro athlete.

CHAPTER 5

Mentors: People Who Care,
Versus People Trying to Get Their Share

Nobody ever said that life would be easy. It isn't easy when you have nothing, for sure. But it certainly isn't easy when you have a lot. It's often hard to differentiate between the people who are trying to get in your pockets and those who are genuinely trying to help. If you could instinctively and instantly know this about everyone you meet, you wouldn't need a book like this. Your favorite advice columnist will not appear in your bedroom to tell you whom to date, whom to love, whom to marry, and how many kids to have. Warren Buffet isn't going to appear in your living room with stock tips. That is the reality for the majority of us.

This is where a mentor can be a great asset.

A mentor may come from any part of your life. Your mentor could be a college professor, a Little League coach, or anyone that sees potential in you. Sometimes mentors find you and sometimes you find them. There is no formula for seeking out someone who will dispense life advice and counsel you in times of need.

It's not unusual to think you have found a mentor, but the relationship doesn't last. There's always that one person that is self-proclaimed mentor whose advice sucks, but you just don't have the heart to tell them. But then, there is that one gem that shines bright like a diamond. Remember, a diamond is first a chunk of coal that undergoes a significant amount of pressure in order to shine brightly. Only few people you meet in life will glow after undergoing life's intense pressure. But once you find your gem, hang on and listen attentively because his or her words will be impactful, turning your little bit of coal into a bright gem.

What Is the Capital of Culture?

For me, the root of a true mentorship lies in cultural capital. The term "cultural capital" was coined in the 1970s by French sociologists Pierre Bourdieu and Jean-Claude Passeron. Cultural capital is the assets a person accumulates that are not necessarily financial or quantitative, assets you cannot necessarily acquire with money alone—like the way to dress or talk; your style and education, for instance. A person with cultural capital can work any room.

Mentorship works in a similar way. It is hard to quantify, and it takes more than money to cultivate the relationship.

A mentor most likely has lived longer than you, and has definitely been successful longer than you have. He is established. Mentors surround themselves with other successful people, and grow from their failures. Your mentors will be able to share their advice on financial capital, but they will also be able to share the most valuable of assets: cultural capital. The closer you become to your mentors the more you will trust their advice.

Are You My Friend or My Mentor?

That's a key question you'll have to ponder with both old and new relationships. Mentors are usually part of a reference group that possesses attitudes, behaviors, and beliefs that will influence you in a positive manner. You don't usually find your mentor within your circle of immediate friends, though the introduction to your mentor often happens organically—or even haphazardly. While your mentor can be your friend, it's not necessarily so. A friend can give you good advice, but that doesn't make them a mentor. Friends and mentors may possess some of the same qualities. Both care about you and have your best interest at heart. However, the person who has equal experience to yours is a friend and the person who has more experience than you is a mentor. Another distinction: A friendship usually has some sort of equal input and output. When friends don't last, it's usually because one person thinks they are giving more than they are getting. Someone feels slighted because he or she is making the greater effort to stay in touch. Sometimes the two go adrift for no apparent reason. A mentorship is much more one-sided, much more didactic: the mentor teaches, the mentee learns.

Some mentors may be a lot older than you, or even younger than you. Their experience and expertise matters more than their age. Mentors give you sound advice when you need it. However, they aren't perfect. We are all flawed in one way or another, and that holds true for mentors. They are not gurus nor are they Zen masters. They can make excellent guides, but they are human—they do not have every aspect of their lives figured out. Yet, they likely have more experience in certain areas, and this is what makes them invaluable.

The mentors that are of value to me, especially in my financial life, are the mentors who see me for who I am off the field. They do not see me solely as a football player, but as a complete person. They encourage me to make educated decisions that have long-lasting positive impacts on my overall financial portfolios. They never tell me what to do, but merely offer suggestions and point out unforeseen risks. When they talk, I listen.

The Periodic Table of Mentors

Chemistry provides a good metaphor for your rapport with mentors. Mentors work much like elements on the periodic table: the reaction of two or more elements together results in the formation of a chemical bond. When one person's strengths can be used to bring out the potential in someone else, the result is powerful, positive chemistry.

On the other hand, not all elements react the same way. Some lose strength when they come in contact with each other; some may not react at all and therefore lack any sort of bond. Each element has a set of qualities that makes it special. For a mentor, this may mean a specific skill set, wisdom, or experience. It's hard to predict the reaction until you test it out.

There are four types of mentors, each unique in their qualities, reliability, and degree of reactivity: Helium (He), Silver (Ag), Gold (Au), and Platinum (Pt).

Helium (He) Mentors

The (not-so) noble gas. The Helium Mentor has ulterior motives. He or she is colorless, odorless, and tasteless. Often, this type is hard to detect because he makes things appear one way when they are actually another. Helium mentors can also be nontoxic. Meaning, they mean well but often give bad advice. They exist only as gas; they are full of ideas, but there is no substance to them. Helium is also the most abundant element in the observable universe. Unfortunately, bad mentors—be they the type with ulterior motives or the type that mean well but just can't seem to give good advice—are far more abundant than good mentors (see Gold and Platinum Mentors).

It's easy to get fooled by the first type of Helium Mentor—the (not-so) noble gas with ulterior motives. These are people trying to get their share. They approach you, and at first it seems like they want to support you, but often they want you to back their own ideas. The goal of a mentor-mentee relationship should not revolve around you investing in their idea. Watch out for people who tell you they want to help, but then spend the rest of your time together talking about themselves, their desires, and *their* dreams.

Helium Mentors typically act from two desires. The first is the need to put your money to work to fulfill their dreams, rather than yours. My dad, for example, was a classic case of this type of mentor.

I should have been wary. When money came into the picture, he wanted to play the father that I never. The relationship between him and I felt forced.

My father had the idea that if you owned your own land, it was a symbol of status and success. This was his dream. My first year in the NFL, I trusted my dad would not steer me in the wrong direction. I was still young, just twenty-two. Everything was new to me. My dad had been talking to a Florida realtor who told him that a piece of land in Cape Coral would be a good investment. The realtor sold me by saying I would be making an excellent investment when, in reality, all she was doing was booking a nice commission fee. My dad and the agent advised me to buy two lots. I lost about $100,000, paying over six times the land's true value. The lesson I learned? I should never have taken my dad's advice because he knew nothing about that specific investment.

Helium Mentors are also likely to be in pursuit of their own business objectives. They often have plans to use your credibility to persuade others to align with them and their ventures. There will always be businessmen trying to persuade you, and your helium mentor, to invest in the hottest deal. Just because a person knows your teammate or relative, doesn't make him credible. What matters most is the quality of a person's service, experience, expertise, integrity, and trustworthiness.

Helium Mentors can easily be identified by their skewing the relationship because they're mainly interested in how you can help them make a business deal. Once I made it to the NFL, I became someone people used to validate their own credibility.

Early on, a friend I knew for about a year offered me an equal part of her share in a hair-care product she was developing. She was posing as a mentor, but she was trying to get me on-board. I thought the idea was cool but not worth my money. I knew nothing about the business, and I wasn't interested in learning about it. She said she had connections with people in China and Europe, and that she would take care of the distributions. In her mind, it was my name, my endorsement, that was going to help sell the product. As part owner, I naturally would want to promote it. With my backing, her product could instantly be exposed to all my Twitter and Facebook friends and followers. These kinds of motives have the potential to land you in a really bad situation. Lesson here? If you have the slightest doubt, sit it out.

The second type of Helium Mentor, the nontoxic type, has good intentions but gives bad advice. Sadly, this was the case with the father of a good high school friend, Nick Monsanto, Sr. This was a man whom I respected and wanted to trust because I loved him, and I knew he really cared about me. He wanted to help; he just didn't have the tools to do it. He had huge deficits in understanding finance and was therefore incapable of dispensing sound business advice. I learned this after I began noticing how he did business. He formed a lot of assumptions that got him into trouble. He often failed to do his homework when making investments, and that wasn't the way I wanted to conduct business.

There are often people close to you that would never hurt you intentionally, but may accidently provide misleading information that causes financial harm. One of the hardest realities a New Money Millionaire must face is saying no to someone who really means well. Failing to do this comes with an expensive price tag—and your resentment will grow with each bad financial experience. Helium mentors may mean well, but that doesn't preclude them from giving bad advice.

Silver (Ag) Mentors

Silver has the highest electrical conductivity of all the metals. A Silver Mentor is someone you may be close to and have known for a long time. Silver also has the highest thermal conductivity of all metals.

The same goes for your relationship with a Silver Mentor—you get along with them well and share similar interests, and they'll look out for you when they see something that is not right. But silver needs a protective coating to avoid tarnishing because it tarnishes quite easily. Silver mentors also tarnish; they tend to lack luster—a degree of cultural capital, for example, and, sometimes, experience.

My Little League coach was a good example of a Silver Mentor. From the start, he always wanted what was best for me and encouraged me to try and work towards my goals. He understood my family situation and my background, which enabled him to give me valuable advice tailored to my circumstance. He also had a healthy and simple philosophy about life: Think, sleep, decide, and let it go.

This might not have been someone who was in the position to give me financial advice, but he was someone I could trust for life advice. He was someone who had my back as a kid, and this continued as I grew older. He called me from time to time, even through my college years, to see how I was doing. Never once did he ask for anything in return. He just wanted to make sure I was on the right path and doing well.

Another Silver Mentor that is critical in my life is Rick Adame, the videographer for my high school football team. I met him my sophomore year, and he quickly became another voice encouraging me to fulfill my potential. His daughter was in my class, and we developed a close friendship. Eventually, he, his wife, Becky, and his daughters became my extended family. They looked out for me when I was a teenager, and today, things haven't changed (It doesn't hurt that Rick's favorite college team is Miami, so he still comes down and visits). He will always call me to have dinner when he's in my neighborhood, and I always have to sneak my credit card to the waiter because Becky still tries to pay. He took care of me for a long time, and I am happy to return the favor now. Now, the mentor and mentee fight over the dinner check.

Other Silver Mentors, in general, could be your church pastors or coaches. Your mentors are the people that emphasize doing things right, instead of doing things right now.

Gold (Au) Mentors

Next to platinum on the periodic table is gold. As a transition metal, Gold Mentors help you manage the chaotic parts of your life and make positive changes towards stability. Gold is also a good conductor of heat; these mentors have a way of igniting the fire in you, seeing to it that your dreams become reality. Also important, gold does not tarnish. These kinds of mentors go the distance and last the test of time. They stand by you through the toughest of times and are built on a solid foundation that's hard to shake.

Like a Silver Mentor, the gold version is someone who guides you without looking for anything in return. If you give him something he's appreciative, but he will never ask. He sees you more as a little brother. He's going to give you advice from the heart.

Jonathan Nash has been as good as gold. Jonathan took me under his wing. As a businessman, his perspective always sheds a bright light on many of the decisions I have to make during negotiations. I've worked on contracts with him for some of my business pursuits, in fact, that is how he took an interest to me. He found out that I was making costly mistakes in many of my current contracts.

With his help, I've learned to negotiate business deals that make sense for me. This often requires speaking to a minimum of three to five different companies at a time when taking on new ventures. This helps me get a feel for the vibe of the company and often allows for comparable comparisons, useful in the negotiation process. With Jonathan's help, I've learned to listen for that Bob Barker voice, ringing in my ear, calling out, "The price is right!" He pushes me to do the due diligence necessary when making a good deal.

Another lesson I've learned from Jonathan is that the most important thing about a contract is being able to get out of it. You need an out clause, an exit strategy, and along with it, a recovery plan. An example: I'm in the process of creating an original comic book. I hired and negotiated a contract with a writer while also pursing an editor that would remain onboard for many future projects. Once I identified the editor, she requested that we work with her writer. I was faced with an important decision. Because I didn't want to lose her as an editor, I had to end the contract with the original writer I hired. Thanks to Jonathon's advice, we had wiggle room in our deal.

Jonathan has been a fountain of information and intelligence. Our relationship runs much deeper than the advice he shares. As an attorney, unlike most of his peers, creating billable hours is not his main priority. Often, many New Money Millionaires are faced with hurdles in unfamiliar territory. It was Jonathan who recommended I hire an expert to oversee business transactions in certain industries, simply to make sure I was not being taken advantage of. Someone like Jonathan is absolutely necessary for the New Money Millionaire.

This is critical. A good mentor will tell you right away when they don't know something, insisting you seek someone who does. They stress the importance of doing things right, forcing you to temper your urge to get things done in a hurry. That said, time is money. Jonathon always ensures I have reasonable checkpoints in place, making sure those working with me are making adequate progress. Problems and delays will occur, but a good mentor will makes sure you don't lose your perspective and panic. Jonathan always advises me to shift my attention away from what I can't do, and focus on what I can do.

Platinum (Pt) Mentors

Platinum is a *catalyst*. A Platinum Mentor is capable of igniting an even faster, stronger fire in you than the Gold Mentor. Your rate of productivity increases exponentially around the Platinum Mentor. Platinum is one of the rarest elements in the Earth's crust. It is also the least reactive metal. Platinum also has a remarkable resistance to corrosion. This mentor is able to withstand the temptations, negative energy, and haters out there polluting the environment. A mentor of this caliber is hard to find.

The best indicator of Platinum Mentors is that they are willing to invest their money along with you. They'll put their own skin in the game. If someone advising me to invest money in something is willing to invest his money alongside me, it gives me an additional sense of trust.

A large part of finding and securing a Platinum Mentor is putting in the hours. Due diligence often means a lot of work, getting a lot of second and third opinions. It's not just about the other person. If you're serious about getting help, Platinum Mentors will be serious about helping you. A successful mentor/mentee relationship works in an interesting way. Mentors need the satisfaction—and it is all they really need—that they're actually helping you. They want to see visible results. That's their gratification.

One of my Platinum mentors is Gary Shiffman. I met Gary while playing for the Detroit Lions. He is white and rich, the dad I never had. The thing I respect most about Gary is his honesty. He is 100 percent transparent; he would never let me get involved in a bad deal. When Gary presents a business proposition to me, there are always options—that's what I like most. In one instance, I wanted to invest in real estate, and Gary presented me with two deals. The first involved investing with an 8 percent yearly return, paid monthly. The other involved investing with a 10 percent yearly return, paid quarterly. Obviously, the one with the higher annual return represented the greater risk.

He considered them both to be fairly safe real estate deals; however, he always reminded me that in any real estate deal I could lose a considerable amount of my investment. I planned to invest a set amount of money—between $100,000 and $300,000. Gary suggested it was better to spread it out over three to five different deals. That way, if one deal went bad, I was potentially making money in the other deals. Gary helped me diversify and spread my risk. I took his advice and invested in both. I'd learned my lesson about putting everything in one basket (Remember, Curt Schilling blew $50 million on a single deal). I'm hopeful that both deals will prove successful, but if not, my chances are better than they would have been if I risked losing it all, like I'd done before when I blindly bought those lots after my dad's advice.

Gary taught me about the fine print of business. You have to read the small type. There are always side effects! He taught me, for example, personal guarantees can go bad, particularly when you sign a personal guarantee for a loan. He gave me a hypothetical situation about a person who is in on a deal for only 20 percent, and the other 80 percent is someone else. If the guy who invested more doesn't pay, a creditor will keep going down the line until he gets his money. Even if you are a minority investor, you can still be on the hook for what your partner owes. Regardless of a personal guarantee, creditors are going to come after you if you are the only one left with money. Creditors will spend their money on attorneys only to go after the ones with the deepest pockets. New Money athletes are certainly in this category. You must understand your entire risk exposure before signing any deal.

Initially, Gary earned my trust when he suggested that I invest a smaller amount in a bank deal that had already doubled since its inception and had the potential to triple. My first reaction was to think, *Man, I should have put in more,* but Gary always said, "There are very few deals—if any—that are guaranteed, so it is better to be surprised in a good way." Every gambler that ever wins a bet says to himself, "I should have bet more." A great Platinum Mentor keeps you in your financial comfort zone. In fact, Gary would tell me about certain deals that had come up but would warn me to stay away from them because of the risks involved. Most important, you need a mentor that will remind you never to jump into a high-risk deal where you cannot afford to lose the entire amount. It is amazing how many athletes and New Money Millionaires disregard this basic tenet.

I think of my Platinum and Gold Mentors as people that I would be okay trading lives with. Remember this: mentors are about relationships that last over a long period of time. Having the right mentor will ultimately save you a lot of headaches and money in the long run. The right financial mentor will always be willing to share the mistakes he's made with you; he will be instructional. They are willing to impart their knowledge along the way, even if it was knowledge that came at a cost to them, even if what they are sharing with you helps you get ahead faster than they did. True mentors are entirely selfless.

Justin Bieber sings, "As long as you love me, I'll be your platinum. I'll be your silver. I'll be your gold." I say, "If you want to mentor me, you gotta be platinum. Silver. Gold." The right mentors can save you from a lot of trouble and hardship, so my advice is that it's well worth the work to seek them out.

CHAPTER 6

From Ballin' to Creditors Callin'

Debit Cards versus Credit Cards—Make the Smart Choice

I'm constantly surprised how many New Money Millionaires have no idea what they're doing when they get their first piece of plastic with their name on the front and a magnetic stripe on the back. Uh-oh. Here comes trouble. As I mentioned earlier in the book, we are a nation of consumers, and the economy is begging us to consume at an increasing pace—on the Internet, at the mall, all day, all night. Did you ever wonder why financial experts are constantly analyzing every detail of our spending habits? They are particularly concerned with what they call "consumer confidence." This is their way of gauging whether we are in the mood to spend rather than save. If consumer confidence is high, it means we're in a good mood, and we're more likely to spend money—especially money we don't have. Bear with me while I tell you what you need to know about these little plastic cards. For some of you, this may be Basic Finance 101, and you don't need to take the course. But I'm guessing it will be a compelling refresher even if you think you know what you're doing.

First, know the difference between debit cards and credit cards. The main difference is the way the card works and where the money comes from. Both allow you to buy goods and services at will. When purchasing with a debit card, money is withdrawn directly from your bank account. When purchasing with a credit card, no money is withdrawn from your bank account, however you will owe money to the credit card issuer at the end of every month. Credit cards come with hefty interest rates and penalties if you do not pay at the end of every billing cycle. MasterCard, Visa, and the like are basically legal loan sharks. The maximum interest rates are set by law on a state-by-state basis, but they are usually very high. Debit cards do not carry a line of credit. The purchases made with a debit card cannot exceed the amount of money in that person's bank account.

Another difference between credit and debit cards is the risk involved. Because they are attached to a bank account, losing a debit card can be very risky. A person does not necessarily need a PIN number to use a debit card and therefore can easily drain a person's bank account, causing extreme problems.

On the other hand, debit cards force discipline. With a debit card, you can't keep swiping when there's no money there. Often, New Money Millionaires don't mess with debit cards because it adds an obstacle to their spending. I know. I was one of them. You're not asking yourself whether you have enough money in the bank to buy your new toys or new designer shoes, you're thinking, *As long as the card isn't declined, we're all good.* And when the MasterCard runs out, you pull out the Visa, until it's time for the American Express, and so on.

Going over the limit happens to everyone at least once. One day, after spending $3000 in one afternoon, I went over my daily debit card limit. It was declined in the store, but luckily I had enough cash and wasn't totally embarrassed in front of my friends and three females.

A credit card swipe is like a dab of soft butter going smoothly on a slice of bread. It feels like "free money" for an instant, and it's easy to make rash decisions in the flick of that swipe. Swoosh. There goes your money. But it isn't free money, and the credit limit looms, as do those high interest rates. Sooner rather than later, the swipes start adding up. Wait till you look at a bill and wonder, *did I really charge all that in February?* Everyone I know says this at one time or another. Credit or debit, you need to put yourself on a budget.

This might sound stupid, but at one point I was spending so much money I was afraid to look at the bills. That's weird, right? But it's true. I remember looking at one of my credit card statements and I was shocked to see I had charged more than $50,000 in one month. This happened while I was playing for the Houston Texans. I never really paid attention to this at the time because I knew other NFL players who were spending nearly twice as much as I. As I got wiser, I was able to look at all of my accounts without fear. But the point is this: know your limit, stick to it, and don't compete with guys who are earning more money than you.

Credit—Use It, Don't Abuse It

In my experience, credit cards are good because they help build your credit history. It sounds counterintuitive, but you cannot get a good credit rating unless you are charging goods and services and paying your cards off on time.

Sometimes, credit cards serve to solve cash-flow problems when you're just starting out. But long term, they set you up for problems, especially if you're not a disciplined spender. Starting out in the NFL, I had a low credit score, but because I was an NFL player I could get credit anytime I wanted. As a New Money Millionaire, I had so many credit cards that I was constantly making payments. When I missed a payment, intentionally or unintentionally, my interest rate went up and my credit score went down. I always ended up paying much more than I intended to pay for any one item. That $120 pair of sneakers quickly becomes $150 or $180 if you're not opening your mail on time.

When I first got to the NFL, All-Pro running back Edgerrin James said to me, "If you can't pay for it in cash, it probably means you don't need it." Initially I didn't understand the true meaning of those words. But the more I thought about it, the more I understood how smart that statement is. At the time, I ignored James's advice. I thought, *you're right, Edgerrin, but I want it.* I had no patience.

Over time, I learned what Edgerrin really meant, and this led me to other lessons. When I started trying to organize my life, financially and personally, I felt that an easy place to start was credit. First, I learned that it is only necessary to have one major credit card. It was something I could, with time, consolidate and control. I cut back on the spending, the number of cars I had, the houses, and, most important, I cut down on the credit cards. With only one credit card, there was only one website to log on to, to check my transactions, one bill to pay at the end of each month, and one grand total I needed to concern myself with paying off. I didn't have to think about adding four totals together anymore.

With four active cards, it had begun to feel like I had four children with hungry mouths to feed, all of them begging for me to help. If one kid was on my arm, the others were tugging at my coattails. When I took too much time with one, another one started to fall through the cracks; there was just no way to keep up with all four in a balanced way. There may be some wealthy people who don't have this problem. But most New Money Millionaires will have a similar experience to mine. The more cards you have, the more your spending can get out of hand. With one card, I was focused and had clarity; less could go wrong.

At the beginning of my career, there were other people managing my money. Bookkeeping was done for me from day one till my sixth year in the pros. Few of us knew how to do this ourselves. It's not like we learned how to do this stuff in high school or in college. Nothing really prepared me for the real world of handling money. When I started watching all of my accounts, it kept me accountable to my spending habits. Now, I don't need to call my financial advisor to know how much I have and how much I owe.

Benefits of Credit Cards if Used Wisely

A credit card can serve a number of positive purposes if not abused. Credit cards may serve well when conducting major transactions. It's not always wise to walk around with $10,000 in cash if you want to make a big purchase. You may very well have the money to pay for the large transaction (and should, if you're going to charge it), but your money might be distributed in various checking, savings, and money-market accounts, so you might not be able to use a particular debit card. In these instances, credit cards with sizeable limits are handy. A second credit card with a large credit limit might be useful if you use it only for large-ticket items. You won't be swiping it every day, and there won't be dozens of charges to scan and verify when you get your monthly bill.

There is also a certain degree of security in credit. For example, American Express has a policy that if something is stolen within a certain amount of time of purchase, a claim can be made. It's a good card to have if you have a dispute with a retailer, as well. They will immediately issue a temporary credit on your balance until the issue is resolved. And they always put the onus of proof on the retailer and not the customer.

Credit cards also provide swifter security against identity theft. It's much easier to make a claim against theft using a credit card than a debit card. If your debit card number is stolen, your bank will sometimes freeze your account, or you will be issued a new card. Getting the money back from the purchases your thief made will take a while, thereby cutting off your personal cash. For this reason, and others, credit cards are your smartest bet for online purchases.

I've become the type of person that likes to feel good about not owing anything to anyone; it reduces my stress level. With no debt, or controlled debt, you don't have to worry about how many people you owe money, when the money is due, or what interest rate that you're getting charged. The list goes on.

In summary, a credit card is good only when you understand your spending limit and stay within it, pay it off every month, on time, and don't use it for cash advances.

Lent Money Is Spent Money—You Mean "Loan," They Mean "Gift"

When you're dealing with a credit card, things are pretty clear-cut. You don't pay, you get charged interest. You don't pay the interest, or fall too far behind on payments, and you get cut off. You get phone calls day and night from creditors, telling you to pay, until you get worn down.

But there are times when credit gets complicated. As a New Money Millionaire, you find yourself on both sides of the credit problem. Sometimes you're the borrower (as in the case of the credit cards), and sometimes you're the bank (as in the case with family).

Suddenly, you're the rich family member, and more often than not, if a rich family member loans capital to a poor relative, that relative will not repay the loan. The family borrower has a flawed mindset: you do not need the money, so you should just *give* it to the one who does. The loan then becomes a gift without you ever realizing it. This is about the time when you start to understand why credit cards have all that fine print when you sign up, and you wonder why you didn't have your family borrowers sign a contract with you.

When it comes to dealing with family, it definitely helps to get some advice from people who have been through similar situations. One thing I learned is that when I gave a family member a loan, I shouldn't expect to get my money back. It was a gift. It's that simple. To analyze it any other way will drive you so crazy you'll never have a good night's sleep again. That's the way it worked in my family and in many of my teammates' families.

Knowing this, I had to be careful of who I lent money to. A good rule, in general: if you can't suffer the loss of losing the money you loan, don't lend it. Beyond that, it's important to evaluate the person you're lending to. Now, I think through any loan before I make it. It's tempting to help out friends and family who are going through hard times and desperate situations, but you must be cautious when dealing with desperation. If you don't catch red flags easily, you run the risk of being emotionally manipulated and played. Ask yourself two questions: "Do they really *need* the loan?" and, "What do you think they'll use the money for?" If you can get honest answers, perhaps you'll lend the money. If not, be aware that this will not be the last request you'll get from that person.

After the Loan, the Paper Chase

I remember loaning a friend a thousand dollars, and it was nothing less than a long headache trying to get the money back. It was a headache that never would have gone away had I not come to terms with the fact that my loan had turned into a gift. He told me that he needed money to help out his girlfriend. He also had a daughter to provide for. I had known him for a few years, and expected him to be more on point than others when it came to paying me back. In fact, I had confidence that he would come through with the money in the end.

Getting repaid wasn't about the amount, I now realize. I became obsessed with repayment merely because it came down to a matter of character. My ego became involved. I didn't want to admit to myself that I had made a bad loan. I would call him, sometimes daily, asking for the money. Most of the time he didn't answer. I would text and call again. The fact that he wasn't responding gave me my answer, but it took a while for me to realize it.

Furthermore, the annoyance continued when he finally answered phone call; he would take the liar's way out, behaving much like the gambler who is in debt to his bookie. "I'll have it for you next week," he'd say. Then a month passed, a year, and then two. Again, my loan was a gift. But I was in denial for a long time. And it was just a waste of energy. Had I written off the thousand as soon as I loaned it to him, I would have said, "Forget giving it back, it's yours."

The requests for money are usually urgent, and the requestor puts you in a spot where it's hard to say no, or even, "Let me think about it." If you stall, bad blood between you and the wannabe borrower starts to flow right away. Your instinct is that it's a bad idea; the borrower's instinct is, *He's hesitating because he doesn't trust me.* Well, you're both right. As soon as I became a New Money Millionaire, I was suddenly a financial fireman, in charge of putting out other people's fires. Everywhere I turned, I faced someone's "emergency." I had to become very selective and learn that sometimes *no* can be the best two-letter word in the English language. I began to reevaluate loan requests, and I learned a better approach.

Without the Wall in Wall Street, You're Left With Only the Street

When helping friends financially, use the Wall Street Approach and not the Street Approach

Street Approach [Strēt ə-prōch] ▶ *n.*
1. Quick to hand out cash without a written receipt or a signed contract.
2. Trusting the borrower to do the right thing with no formal structure of accountability.
3. Banking on a person's word and loyalty.
4. Borrower thinks you owe them for something, so he or she doesn't have to pay you back.
5. Borrower doesn't think he or she has to pay you back because you have money and he or she doesn't.

On Wall Street everything is recorded: There is a paper trail for all transactions. It's in black and white. This is the same approach I learned to use when dealing with loans. That means drafting up a simple contract between yourself (in my case, Bank of Buchanon) and the borrower. The Street Approach would be handing out cash—$500 here, $1,000 there—and banking on the word and loyalty of your borrower.

The paperwork shouldn't seem overly formal and unnecessary. Be like a bank, just for these occasions. Does Citibank take your word to pay back your mortgage? No. So you shouldn't either. When it comes to money, get it down on paper. Create a workable system as well as a litmus test that works for you. This is one that has served as my guide to avoid falling back into the Street Approach. Before I loan money to someone, I ask myself:

1. Does the person have an addiction? If the answer is yes, I do not loan the money. If no, move on to question 2.
2. Did the person create the situation because of foolishness? If the answer is yes, I do not loan the money. If no, move on to question 3.
3. Does this person have the ability to help themselves, yet asks for money again and again? If the answer is yes, I do not loan the money (If I do, I'm enabling them.). If no, move on to question 4.
4. Was there an act of God or situation beyond their control and they really need your help—and you can help (Typically, this is not a recurring event.)? If the answer is yes, *and* I am in the position to help, I consider helping. If the answer is yes and I am not in the position to help, I do not loan the money (I cannot afford to replace everyone in my neighborhood's roof after a hurricane.). If the answer is no, I don't make the loan.

Here is a situation where I was put in the position of trying to help a woman friend from my hometown of Ft. Myers. We knew each other well and I wanted to help her out in a loving and caring way. In fact, I wanted to play the role of big brother. One night we had one of our many discussions about business. She wanted to pick my brain because she knew I had been involved in many investments, some good, some not so successful. In order to encourage her, I mentioned several excellent businesswomen who started with nothing and became very wealthy and successful. Women like Sara Blakely (who introduced the Spanx undergarments) and J. K. Rowling (who created the Harry Potter novels and franchise). I mentioned *How I Made My Millions* episodes from CNBC.

Remember, we were only friends, and I was not looking for anything in return. She had an idea for a product, and I thought it was terrific. After several discussions, she said she wanted me to be an equal partner. I declined because I was too busy with my other investments, and I couldn't devote enough time to be a 50/50 partner. I wanted to help her on an informal basis. She still insisted on giving me half of the business, and in turn, we would split the expenses evenly.

Her idea was to come up with a beauty cream that helps women maintain a youthful appearance. I didn't know anything about these industries, and I didn't know if such a product had a commercial future. I was still willing to help and devote time and effort to seeing her idea come to fruition. For example, I came up with the name for the product.

Five or six months went by, and she met a guy from New York who apparently was working on a similar idea. Eventually, they decided to work together because he was going to finance the development of the product. When we started doing business together we never had a written contract. We only had a verbal agreement.

But now, she had a new partner who financed her project. When she had any disagreements with this new business partner, I was her sounding board. She would tell me everything, and I would be a calming influence, explaining that everything would turn out okay.

I told her it would be different if her New York partner was spending her money, but he was spending his money. But then, out of no where, she claimed I wasn't doing enough to help her—despite me taking all of her calls and giving her advice when she asked for it. I even talked to the guy in New York after everything was vetted by lawyers and in contract form. I was loyal to my friend.

But, she felt that I no longer deserved to be her equal partner. I felt this tension coming because she started thinking about the money instead of making a great product. Because I valued her friendship and her idea, I gave her three options to change the agreement—all increasing her stake and decreasing mine. She agreed to 80-20. I was okay with this. But the very next day she called me and said she needed me to do more work.

I couldn't believe it. I'm like, *WTF are you talking about?* But she was serious. Things were starting to heat up. She appointed a different lawyer to draft our contract, not my usual attorney that we used to draft her contract with her New York partner. The new contract deemed me responsible for more work than we initially agreed upon.

I asked my attorney to take these new responsibilities out of the contract, and my friend got mad. I told her I had given in on the percentage and resented being asked to do more, not less. She then came back and said I would only get paid if and when the company was sold. My reaction was, "You mean to tell me that if this company starts making money tomorrow, you are not going to pay me a cent?" She said, "Yes, that's right." I was thinking the following: *If this company starts to make a lot of money in the next five years and then isn't sold but then files for bankruptcy, then I'll lose my investment.*

Worst-case scenario, I lose money trying to help a friend. Using legal advice at the beginning of a business deal is much less expensive than having to use it to get out of one or defend against a lawsuit. Always do things the Wall Street way.

CHAPTER 7

Lifelong Learning Leads to Increased Earning

More About Bad Business Deals—and How to Avoid Them

I'll begin this chapter with a somewhat pathetic confession of just how crazy I treated some of my new money. Yes, as you've read earlier, in the beginning of my career I blew large amounts of cash while having a good time with my Fun Friends. That was just pure spending. It was a habit I grew out of. But the following story is worse because I talked myself into the notion that there was a possible upside to it. Sort of a Fun Friend Investment.

It all started when I was kid. I made a promise to one of my childhood friends, CB, and told him that when I make it to the NFL, I would try and give him a chance at making it in the rap game. I knew deep down that this might be a waste of money because I had no real business knowledge. I probably went through between $150,000 and $200,000, and all I can say about this experience is that I had fun in a stupid way.

Of course, I was in way over my head, but I wanted to give CB a chance to realize his dream and become a star because I had great aspirations for him. I wanted him to be known globally. There was another friend, Dee—a budding Puff Daddy—who wanted to become a music producer. He really thought he was a young Sean Combs.

Being a pro athlete gave me the chance to meet many local entertainers: Princess, Small Change, Mikey, and the late Corner Pocket, just to name a few. We created mix tapes and passed them out in my Hummers (which were loaners from dealers at the time). I was living large, as you can imagine. I had a three-bedroom condo for the record crew. We created a makeshift studio in one of the closets in a room at the DoubleTree Grand Hotel in Miami.

None of this ever worked out. What I should have done was put some money in an account, perhaps $100,000. I should have made sure Dee, who I called Poof Daddy because he wanted to be Puff Daddy, and CB did an internship with a legitimate record label for about a year or two before I began writing bigger checks. I could have tried to make sure they were introduced to people in the music business that could offer real advice. At the time, we were around a lot of sharks that were just taking advantage of me as a New Money Millionaire. Today, the NFL has a music workshop that might have been helpful if available in 2003. But looking back, it was an expensive entertainment and business lesson.

The music business wasn't the first, or the last, time I failed to think wisely about business decisions.

In March 2002, a few months before the NFL draft, another player and I were approached about a business deal in the car industry. I had been offered many other business deals, but I can't say I' put any real thought into them. But this seemed different. This was an offer that involved a free trip to Atlanta. My view at the time was, "If it works out, cool; if it doesn't, I head back home." What was the risk in kicking the tires?

The man that approached us wanted to use our names to get a $1 million loan, and in return he offered us a percentage of his profit. We had never stepped on a pro football field, yet we already had currency. In his mind, our names equaled money. He flew us to Atlanta and requested to meet at the strip club he owned to discuss the deal in further detail. He greeted us and asked, "What are you all drinking? What girls can I get you?"

It went from liquor to women just that fast. He wanted us to know that we could have whatever we wanted and as much of it as we could handle. It was tempting. He was attempting to exploit our weaknesses—alcohol and women—to try and persuade us to invest in his company. But he was being sketchy about the details. He might have been posing as a businessman—the owner of a car lot and strip club—but he was still running his business like you do in the street: all style and no substance. My friend and I were too green to pick that up at the time. We'd heard negative rumors about him, but we didn't think twice because everything checked out on the surface. We were about to fall into his trap and invest with him. We failed to notice that a Financial Molester was grooming us. We could have made the mistake of cosigning for the loan, not knowing where the money was really going. In the end, if the loan went bad, we would be on the hook for the unpaid balance.

Financial Molester [fə-nan(t)-shəl mə-les-tər] ▶ *n.*

1. One *whose financial interests comes be*fore your interests.
2. When your money is gone, so is he or she.
3. Often found double-dipping; the one that dips twice into the cheese before taking another nacho.
4. Adept at spending your money.
5. Can view you as a meal ticket; when you get paid, they feel they should get paid.
6. Of or pertaining to financial advisor, broker, family friend, etc.

When my friend and I woke up the next morning, both of us had missed calls from advisors working for our agents, warning of the bogus deal and the repercussions of us signing the contract. The thing that I took away from that experience was that we had almost gotten involved with something that put us at risk of losing a lot of money (money that we technically didn't have) just because we'd had a little fun dangled in front of us.

The other lesson I learned was that, in business, you must dig beneath the surface to get to the real grit of the deal. This deal, for example, looked fine at first glance. Receiving a percentage of a business owner's profits just for him using your name sounded like a good deal. But when you started unpacking the crate, it was a bad deal. I hadn't considered the possibility of him leaving me hanging and responsible for the loan.

At the time, I just listened to my friends, but what I really needed was a mentor. My hypothetical mentor would have suggested that I talk with my financial advisor, pick his brain, hear his reasoning; this way, I would be learning and more prepared for the next time a similar idea came across my desk. It's a lot like learning to fish instead of taking a fish someone gives you when you're hungry. If you learn to fish, you'll never go hungry again. If you just take the fish and eat it, you'll quickly satiate yourself, but the next time you're hungry, you might not have someone around to hand you another freebie.

The guy reacted cool, but not rudely when we told him we weren't going through with the deal. He never asked us for anything else. All his pitch cost him was paying for a night of extravagant living for two. That was a risk he'd made on a potential investment—the women and alcohol were already part of his one of his businesses, and a small cost in terms of the potential payoff. Today, in fact, I probably would not even take the plane ticket.

So here is a good suggestion: It's a very good idea to have a financial advisor around during those first few years after coming into a lot of money, at least until you can find a mentor who doesn't need you as a client. There is always the risk of being taken advantage of by financial advisors. After all, they are in business as well. Many New Money Millionaires don't have the knowledge, or the time, to make decisions and manage their investments on a day-to-day basis. It's best to do your homework and hire a good advisor—he or she will save you money, time, and a lot of tossing and turning down the line. Buyer beware: just because someone is a certified financial advisor doesn't mean he won't knowingly or unknowingly give you bad or misleading information.

From Investors to Financial Molesters

My first financial advisor was someone I met at school. When he graduated, he joined an NFL-endorsed financial advisor company. He was working with a lot of the guys I knew, guys that were coming into new money, just like me, so it made sense to go with him.It was an easy decision.

But easy isn't always good—this relationship only lasted six months. I severed all ties with him when I found out that he'd led me to sign an insurance policy that provided catastrophic injur*y insurance on my body if I were to be injure*d in a game, unable to play football ever again. The insurance itself wasn't a bad idea. The problem was that he was part owner of the insurance company he was advising me to sign with. This created a conflict of interest. Obviously, he didn't have my best interest in mind.

This guy collected two or three premiums over the course of a year for the insurance company. One payment was for $34,000. Essentially, the financial advisor was capitalizing on the money he got from the percentage I owed him for making the transaction with him, as well as from the transaction itself because the insurance company was partially his. That's what I call double-dipping; I was grossly overcharged for this standard protection, and I wasn't the only one he was doing this to. It was later uncovered that the company he worked for was making unsuitable investment recommendations to several NFL players. I'd gotten out just in time.

All signs pointed to bad news with this particular advisor. I should have seen it earlier. He'd been out of school and in the business for less than five years, and yet he was living better than any of his NFL clients. For someone so young, this would mean he was making incredible investments with astronomical returns.

It was too good to be true (The old cliché applies here: if it sounds too good to be true, it probably is). He was working the back ends of deals constantly; every transaction he made, he got a kickback. If he didn't get a kickback, he would counsel you not to do the deal, even if it was a good deal. A part of me knew something shady was going on, but at the same time, I didn't know if that was just what smart financial advisors did—make money on both ends. I didn't yet understand the concept of double-dipping.

I was at least savvy enough to begin asking to see timely statements from him. He was never forthcoming with a lot of information, but even this small request was conveniently dodged. One of my colleagues had a weird feeling about him, just as I did, so he said he was going to go check it out. My colleague came back to me and said, "Man, you won't believe what this man just said. He tried to give me money to come back and tell you everything is fine." That's when I knew my gut had been right; he was a Financial Molester—not someone giving me sound, objective financial advice.

Do not to pick a financial advisor that only deals with athletes. They will claim they are specializing, but it is far too limiting. Also, it is important to do your homework on financial advisors. Your friend's recommendation alone is not enough. You need to examine the details before you make any decision. This doesn't mean you don't respect the person that gave you the advice; it just means you're being cautious, safe, and smart. That financial advisor may be good for your friend, but not for you. Just as there are people that want to use you to enhance their credibility, you shouldn't choose an advisor if he tries to name-drop another famous client simply to win your signature.

Get a Good Financial Advisor, Not a Conniver

The next financial advisor I worked with had a clientele base that was similar to me—they'd all come into new money and were very busy people. At this point, I was wrapping up my first NFL season with Oakland. This new advisor put a system in place to pay my bills on time and ensured that the transactions I was involved in were fair and honest, especially if there was a third party involved.

But in terms of the long haul, the advisor told me that I didn't have enough money to make any serious investments. "I'm working with one NBA player that is able to put anywhere from $5 to $10 million into a deals, and you just aren't there yet." In other words, he was telling me I didn't have enough money to invest.

Realistically, I had between a quarter million dollars to a half million dollars to invest. I thought, *you mean I can't invest $50,000 in a deal where someone else is investing $5 million?* That didn't seem logical.

It may not have been multimillions, but it surely was enough to make an investment in something that could potentially increase my net worth. Whereas some advisors are too liberal with your money, having you spend it and invest too much of it, this guy was far too nearsighted He couldn't wait for me to get to a bigger salary level. He was too busy with people that had more money than I. Meanwhile, he had my money sitting in a simple savings account, gaining minimal returns that didn't even keep pace with inflation. What does this mean? If the bank or money-market account is paying 1 or 1.5 percent, and annual inflation is 2.5 or 3 percent, you are losing money. Your principal may not be at risk, but the buying power of your dollar is diminishing.

After a few years, I decided to leave him because my money was not growing. I knew I should be exploring more lucrative investments. In a sense, I felt I was wasting my time. Why did it take me so long to sever my relationship with him? Yes, I could have fired him sooner, but, to his credit, he did a good job managing my bills. He just didn't maximize my money, which was the next step I wanted to make.

At all times during your fiscal education, you should be continually monitoring your financial advisor and noting all he is doing for you, as well as what he is not doing. For example, at one point I had an advisor that was doing nothing but paying my bills. Do you really need a financial advisor to write checks and mail them to your creditors? Probably not. You can do this for yourself. A lot of New Money Millionaires, especially athletes, insist on hiring a financial advisor right away because 1) they are rich (for the moment) and 2) they think it is part of the prestige package. *Everyone else has one; I should too,* they think.

When a financial advisor is charging you to oversee your stock and bond portfolio, you must understand how they get paid. Usually they earn 2 percent per year of "money under management." (Big hedge-fund managers with reputations on Wall Street often charge "two and twenty," meaning 2 percent plus 20 percent of the yearly profits you made.)

So, if you start with $500,000 and end a year at $550,000, they will charge you $11,000. You have to look at it this way. If they tell you to expect an 8 percent return on your portfolio, ask yourself if that return is "net of fees" or not. If he earns 10 percent, then you only really earned 8 percent. Also, if they lose you money, they still get paid.

There is one more thing you should be fully aware of when you find a financial advisor who is very good, honest, up front, and invests your money wisely with strategies toward your future and your retirement. The advisor (and any broker) always gets paid "up front." He's getting fees either through transactions or quarterly or yearly management fees. These are transparent, and there's nothing irregular about this. But your money (and profits) is "on paper." If it's in a retirement fund, it's not usable until you are fifty-five or fifty-nine and a half years old (unless you need the money earlier, and then you pay a 20 percent penalty to the government, plus applicable federal, state, and local taxes) to get access to it. Until you withdraw that money—until it becomes "cash"—you must think of it as a hard asset that's hard to get. It will be good for your financial education. If you are using a financial advisor who has a small client list and not a huge amount of money under management (sometimes an advantage because you'll get personalized service), then you might ask to see his portfolio. Make sure he is investing in the same companies that he is putting you in.

My suggestion is to park a large chunk of your capital in a reputable bank. Leave the money in cash accounts until you find a good advisor, even if the accounts don't earn a lot in interest. You will have time to learn and figure out what you want to do with the money in terms of investing. Meanwhile, you can write checks on this account or make wire transfers to pay bills. If you manage your own investments, you can get free advice from the bank as long as you keep a certain minimum level of money in your accounts (I'm assuming a New Money Millionaires will automatically qualify at most big banks). Some advisors at big financial institutions do not work on commission (salary only), this means they have no vested interest in what financial products you buy. They won't "push" anything on you just because they're going to earn a fee.

Brokers Who Make You Broker

Brokers are like the candy *Now and Laters*. Brokers get paid now, their clients get paid later (but only if the clients are lucky and the brokers are good). Instead of working solely with a financial advisor, I decided to work with big financial institution with a well-known wealth-management company and a stellar reputation. I thought that working with a large company that specializes in brokerage could help me more so than my previous financial advisor. But there's a great deal to be wary of in terms of big brokers, as well.

Brokers are supposed to have the expertise and knowledge to guide you without a conflict of interest. But, as with financial advisors, this isn't always the case.

The first broker I worked with came recommended through an NFL function I attended. I remember having several conversations where I said, "I need you to be honest." His response was always, "This is all I know." He might not have been dishonest, but he wasn't telling me the whole story. Not every broker will give you full disclosure. He was doing what he was told. Whether it was bad advice or good advice, he was following orders from someone higher up. In the end, you are left with an underling who is simply recommending what the company analysts are touting. Your broker may not even know that he's dispensing bad advice.

Despite the broker's *good* advice, he lost me a lot of money. Typically brokers make their living from fees, selling financial products and commissions based on the number of trades they make, regardless of whether you make money or lose money. They are legal bookmakers (Think about a bookmaker who is taking bets on the Super Bowl. He doesn't care which team wins because he is getting a piece of the handle—10 percent of all the losing bets or 5 percent of the entire action.).

Funding Someone Else's Dream

Finding the right balance of financial advice isn't always easy. In 2008, my seventh season in the NFL coincided with the stock market crash and subsequent housing crisis. This was about the time I decided to take my money from my current broker and find a new wealth-management firm. I was uncertain of whether or not the company would be able to get me back to where I was before the crash. The firm was reputable, but despite the company's stability, and the government's willingness to do what it could to help the company recover from the crash, I only had $500,000 left in that account. I simply felt uneasy. I wavered between reconstructing the model I'd worked with earlier—a combination of financial advisor and broker or working solely with a broker.

One of my life lessons cost me $1.6 million, due to a few ill-advised and rushed decisions. The first decision was made directly because of my own desire to recoup losses I'd had in the stock market. But I ended up losing more money when I invested in someone else's idea because I thought it had potential. Yet, I didn't have an established mentor who could objectively help me think about the venture—that is, to help me evaluate the pros and cons and also the quality of the management team.

The year 2009 was coming to an end, the stock market had not made many strides, but my broker at the time felt strongly about me investing another $500,000 in a company working on an idea to improve the current automotive security system that I had already invested in. The initial $500,000 was for the purpose of helping a startup company that had a good chance of becoming very successful. My broker pushed me to write another half-million-dollar check. He said they needed additional financing to finish the final phase before the product and system could be launched.

The owner flew to see me while I was still playing. In retrospect, I should have been more wary. I thought their coming to my door was simply a respectful way to treat an investor. What I didn't know then was they were already entering into a panic mode as their capital was already spent or drying up. I should have seen their being overly concerned for my next investment as a red flag.

But I loved the project they were working on. I thought that it had tremendous potential. But this was their dream, not mine. And, while I was close to the deal and felt very strongly about the idea, I felt a real lack of involvement in the business decisions they made. A silent investor is just that; the owners want you to remain silent. I was blinded by the potential and failed to see that management— namely, the person behind the idea—was terrible. He was very flashy with money; he would talk about how he had so much success in the past and this would be no different.

I ended up investing more than I should have. If I'd had a Platinum Mentor at the time, perhaps he could have helped me cut my losses or helped me see that this company was a long shot at best.

There is still some hope that this idea will come to fruition, but there's only a tiny chance of success. At some point I will write off the losses.

It took me three $500,000 checks to realize their management team was bad. When you have a dream, you need to step back and ask yourself if it is something you can do on your own, or if you need to have someone else do it for you. Looking back, the guy who headed the operation was blind to his own inadequacies as a businessman. Regardless of how great his idea was, he needed to recognize his own strengths and weaknesses. He should have turned the managerial reins over to someone else (This is frequently the case with many new products or new companies. The visionary has no clue how to manage, so he hires someone who does.). This is a common, recurring scenario in business, especially when companies grow and go public. If a company is fortunate, the board of directors sees this and votes to make a management change.

Here's what I should have done. I should have proposed to give them $500,000 on the condition that I receive a greater percentage of the profit or piece of the company. I could have incentivized their performance by creating a map. As they accomplished certain items on a checklist, in a manner and quality that met my approval, then I would have continued to invest more money.

The lesson here is this: you should never assume that when you invest in a company that they are going to do the right thing. You need to perform due diligence on the management team and research on the idea. In the end, you should only invest what you can afford to lose.

At the time, I felt like I was making the right decision. The broker advised me to invest more than my initial $500,000. I trusted this guy's judgment because I had originally given him $100,000 to invest and he produced good returns. In this $100,000 investment, I made it clear that I wanted to be notified immediately if the balance dropped below $70,000. Eventually, my account dipped under $70,000, and I didn't realize until it was down to 70 to 80 percent of the starting figure. I didn't receive a single phone call (Today, you can do this yourself electronically by simply putting a "stop loss" figure on any equity in your portfolio. When it falls to a certain number, it will automatically issue a sell order on the stock).

I made the mistake of trusting our verbal agreement that he would notify me. I never got it in writing because I felt confident that he understood. I haven't seen the money since. When I confronted him, his response was, "Everything is going to be okay, give it some time."

But time is money. I didn't have time, and, after dealing with this broker, I didn't have my money. When you invest or select a broker, the process should be a thorough vetting and selection process followed by weekly monitoring and reporting. One of your first questions should be: Does the broker have any past complaints on file at the NASD, SEC or ancillary regulatory agencies? I failed to maintain adequate financial surveillance of my investment, and it cost me dearly.

I thought I was doing something that made sense. Truthfully, I made the decision to give the $500,000 loan after the initial million I'd invested in the automotive security system because of something I observed in a mentor I trusted. My mentor's situation was different because he was the one running and controlling the day-to-day business. I was only an investor in this particular company. It is true that you sometimes need to invest more than the initial amount—but not as a response to a company's desperation.

I knew my mentor granted a loan to a project he was overseeing. Investing more in the business was right for him at the time, not me, because he was putting his own sweat equity into it as well. I didn't ask the questions to learn why it was right for me. I only observed. Knowing the right questions to ask is critical to making the right decision. There are no stupid questions at this point; you are learning. Ask the questions that are right for you and your particular investment portfolio. Because I skipped the questions, I made a decision that may have been right for my mentor but wrong for me.

It wasn't until much later that I learned two things about the company my broker had me invest in. It was the same company many of his other clients were investing in, and it was a company that was not doing well. I was setup. He used my name to give his other clients hope: "Hey, sit tight. This company is turning around. Phillip Buchanon, the NFL player, is making an investment in it." He got paid, I got played.

I made my final $100,000 mistake when I got antsy and thought I outsmarted the system and found a way to get paid in two ways. I invested $100,000 in another company that was helping the company I initially invested in. I thought that if the second company was the key to getting the first company started, then it was a win-win situation. But it only made matters worse. I made this last $100,000 bet because I thought the second company's management team was better than the original one, and this would rescue the original investment.

In short, I confused playing sports and making money. I didn't realize this until I remembered hearing Steve Rogers from the Kellogg School of Management speak. He put it this way, "In the business world it's okay to be on the sideline and wait for the right pitch." I am so used to doing whatever I can to get on the field, because that was the only way to get your stats up and ultimately up the zeros on your paycheck. The game of business is different. I thought my game plan as a football player would work for business. I didn't realize that it was okay to watch and wait for the right opportunity. I rushed into some of these decisions thinking that it would get my money stats up, but the pitch wasn't right for me.

Continuum of Dreams

The brokers I dealt with represent two ends of the broker continuum. On one end there are conservative brokers. These brokers take orders from their higher-ups, give what they think to be safe advice, and follow rules to the letter. Conversely, there are those that are risk takers. They are the go-against-the-grain brokers. They are willing to explore different options and be innovative in their investment approaches. Instead of taking orders from the higher-ups, they may be challenging the higher-ups to consider a new way of thinking. There is a greater risk to working with these brokers, yet there is also the chance for a larger gain. Regardless of the type of broker you end up choosing, understand that the end result can still lead to a loss of money. For me, it was the luck of the draw. I drew two bad ones. Beware of those brokers who are hard-selling you the next "hot stock" or initial public offering. They are getting paid to tout these new issues. They get paid whether you win or lose money on the deals.

When it comes to investing in liquid equities—that is, the stock market—you can do everything "right" and still lose money. On the other hand, plenty of people who keep their money in safer index funds or mutual funds see healthy gains when the overall economy is doing well. Robust markets usually mean that the rising tide lifts all boats.

When you are determining which type of broker to do business with, there are two things to consider. First, how much money do you have to risk? This is determined by how much money you would be comfortable living without if it was all lost. Second, did you do your homework? In my case, my former broker and I met through a business deal. He seemed trustworthy, but in reality, he wasn't. If you are considering working with a go-against-the-grain broker, look at their past successes and failures. How much success has this broker found? Maybe even more important, how many failures did he incur? I didn't do my homework, so I didn't pass the class. I didn't examine the details behind his strategy or theory; I simply trusted that his "good choices" would be winning moves.

When I lost a great deal of money in 2008, my trust in investing eroded. You need to have a plan. I didn't have one. My strategy was extremely short-term. I just wanted to extricate myself from a bad situation. Had I made a plan to recover the money I had lost, perhaps I would have thought twice about pursuing the guy that approached me for quick gains. If I disciplined and had a plan, I might have said, "Hey, I'm heading in this direction for the next five years, so let me take your card, and maybe I'll contact you then."

You can get lucky on a get-rich-quick scheme, but it's extremely unlikely. In my case, I was like a desperate gambler. Life is not that simple.

Only Make Exchanges in Platinum, Gold, or Silver

Once, a good friend's father recommended I allow a relative to assist me with making sure my bills were paid, even though it was someone he openly admitted he was not comfortable doing business with. He said that it was hard to do business with family. Well, I listened, and he took $100,000 from me.

This is where Gold and Platinum Mentors come in. I found that if you can find a Platinum Mentor and you have the time to learn and invest properly, it could make having a financial advisor or broker irrelevant. Platinum Mentors can help you exist without either. You need to have a good mentor in place for advice, and for those moments when something goes wrong—you need that person to turn to.

At the time, I had good friends, but they weren't mentors. They were people that had my back but weren't capable of helping me sort through my next financial decision. I needed someone to be sure that I was thinking rationally and not emotionally. I was forced to do what I thought was best without much real guidance.

Public Life versus Private Strife

For me, it is important to be able to call my own shots when it comes to investing. To Paraphrase Snoop Dogg, "With my mind on my money and my money on my mind." No one wants to receive a phone call from a financial advisor saying that you've lost all your money. In both of my situations, someone else was making decisions. In order for the power to shift back to me, I needed more education. I went back to school and finished my degree from the University of Miami.

Take it from me: Keep your money in basic investments until you mature. Make sure you fully understand every investment you make. Don't invest until you have solid mentorship, solid business partnerships, and a clear vision. You might need to wait several years, depending on your financial maturity. Initially, I recommend allocating the lion's share of your assets to conservative, established asset classes. This way the focus is on accumulating steady investment yields versus highly speculative schemes. And this allows you to keep your eye on earning a bigger paycheck.

Listen and Learn

I learn a lot from just having a conversation with other people, especially those whose intellect I respect. I always make time to talk to people. You can walk away with at least one important thing from any conversation you have. Whenever you are talking with people, you need to listen. Listen more, talk less, and observe. By talk less, I mean listen 80 percent of the time and speak only 20 percent. Not just listen, but hear and absorb.

Talk time is important and it's easy. The point of these conversations is to get to know the other person better than they know you. Don't be afraid to ask questions. The point of a question is to get an answer, and usually the answer will help you gain knowledge. If it doesn't, then you can at least say you had a good conversation.

The King James Bible

I think the one modern-day athlete who got it right is LeBron James. Yes, he's got a lot going for him, but what I really noticed is this:

not only is his financial management sound, but so is his overall life management. Not a bad thing to say about a guy who never went to college, right?

I mentioned the risk of Historical Friends, family members, financial advisors, Adult Abusers, and so on. Yet, LeBron's family and friends have managed his life. Here's why it worked: LeBron made them all seek training. He made sure they were properly prepared, on a schedule where they became experts in their newly allotted roles. He figured out which friends and family members were willing to take the hard route by learning and growing. Now he has built a solid foundation around him of childhood friends and family that help him maintain his King James status. His situation is unique, of course, because he only has to worry about his next game—and not his investments. He had enough good people in his life that were willing to learn and do the worrying for him. Many people have one or the other—good people that are not willing to learn or bad people that'll learn and then take your money. LeBron figured this out right away.

For me—since I couldn't trust family—I eventually learned that reputable banks were just as capable of helping me pay my bills as any financial advisor. They were also highly trained in their field, unlike the family and friends that claimed to be experts. I recommend splitting your money between two banks—one big bank and one small bank. Having money in an international bank makes it easy to access cash from anywhere, for instance. When you have money in two banks, it gives you some leverage to negotiate when you get ready to finance your house and pay a mortgage or buy a new car. Make sure your banker always knows you can go elsewhere to seek a better deal.

Ideally, I was looking for a self-made millionaire that knew how to handle his money. I wanted to work with someone that made money from scratch, not because they had professional athletes paying them fees that would enable them to live a millionaire lifestyle.

I wanted someone who was growing financially and holistically. I thought that if I allied with someone who took nothing and made it into something, they would be able to advise me on how to do the same. Now I have a number of different people who help me monitor my money. Whether it is close family, friends, or a mentor giving me advice, I am still in total control of my money.

I started to operate under the mentality that if you can't pay it in cash, then you probably don't need it. This is a difficult mind-set to have, but it pays dividends. When weighing a decision, I'll talk to myself. "Okay, I want to buy this car, but would I still feel comfortable paying cash for it?" I'll ask myself. If you wouldn't feel comfortable living after that purchase, then it's really nothing you need. If you can't pay for any large asset in cash (cars or houses), without it hurting your bank account, you probably don't need it. Look at yourself as a business. Have fun, but be smart. Even if you finance your purchase with debt, you may eventually pay two to three times its original value because of the interest payments (Loan disclosures will tell you how much interest you pay over a period of time. It's always a lot more than you think.).

Today, I watch all my accounts; I manage everything. Do not be oblivious to the deposits and withdrawals going in and out of your accounts.

Keep a regular eye on all of your investments. If it's a long-term private investment, then you need to keep tabs on a regular basis. Check in monthly with your contacts, even more often if necessary. If it's in the stock market, spend a few minutes a day checking your gains and losses. Educate yourself so you can understand when an equity moves on general economic news or if it's the specific holding itself. Learn how your money is behaving. It will not behave itself; you must be a strict disciplinarian.

CHAPTER 8

Love and Lust
(You Better Know the Difference)

The Family You Choose

This is one of those chapters where you will hear things you may have heard before, but I'm here to remind you. There are all kinds of women, all kinds of relationships, all kinds of family situations, and I'm sure you've experienced good ones, bad ones, and those that fall in between. When it comes to love and lust, you have to think clearly. This isn't always easy. In matters such as these, we often act first and analyze later. You must reverse the order whenever possible.

Love and lust cause us to think irrationally. That does not mean you shouldn't fall in lust or fall in love. Love is more than physical sex; It's also an emotional and spiritual connection. While, on the other hand, lust is primarily limited to a physical, sexual attraction. There is the family that raises you, the one you're born into, and then there's the one you choose: your wife, your partner, and eventually your children (though you just raise them, you don't really choose them). This new family, just like the old one, can be dangerous territory for the New Money Millionaire.

Not Happily Ever After, but Happily Never After

Polls, studies, and anecdotal evidence suggest that the divorce rate for NFL players is anywhere between 60 to 80 percent, roughly 10 to 30 percent higher than the national average. So for every four marriages, it's likely that three will end. Just having the job means you're away from home more than the typical working male head of household. If you're a husband playing in the NFL, you are potentially away from your wife four to six months out of the year. It might look like you're choosing work over your family, but it's your work that is bringing in the dough that keeps the family rolling. For those with shaky marriages, the long period of separation can be the cause of household tension.

Other, more happily married couples get into a routine during the season; they learn how to support each other in their absences, be it physically or mentally. But even with these couples, the dynamic often changes when an athlete's professional career is over and the roles and rules that once worked so well no longer apply. Once an athlete retires, everything changes. His routine, by definition, changes dramatically, and it impacts the family. Overnight, the couple is living together 24/7, something they might never have done before. For the not-so-happily married, what happens when there's no longer a countdown to leave for Organized Team Activities? Plenty of healthy, family-oriented football players say to me, "Phil, man, I can't wait to get a break." And by "break," they mean go back to work, to practice, to the grueling physical activity that defines their lives.

When you're away at least half of the year, you might fall into the role of provider—someone who works and sends money home. You also take a certain kind of freedom for granted. When you're back home, however, expectations change. If you are going to be late for dinner, you have to call; you have to start picking up the kids from school, showing up at the school play, "doing your part" to ensure domestic tranquility.

You and your spouse might have different opinions about what constitutes your "free time." You might see it as a break from a long and arduous physical season—or entire career, if you're retiring—in sports. She might see it as time to fill, time to help around the house, time to help with the kids. She's going to want you to fulfill her needs.

Ultimately, it's hard to anticipate how the dynamic of your relationship will change and how it will impact your marriage. It's sad to see couples that work so well together end their relationships because they are unable to adjust to life after a professional sports career ends. They can't adjust to living together 24/7.

Then, there is maturity. At age twenty-two or twenty-three, marriage looked a lot different than at twenty-eight or twenty-nine, when the average NFL player's career ends. I'm not saying it isn't possible to stay together after you retire, but I'm also not saying that the "till death do us part" marriage is going to be easy for the New Money Millionaire. It's tough, and the statistics prove it. Many couples do not figure it out, and this is simply another part of the New Money Millionaire puzzle. Marriage is not impossible, but even when it works, from what I've seen, it takes time, analysis, and patience.

Timing is everything. I have never been married because relationships have not occurred at the right time. It could have been the right women but the wrong time or the wrong women at the right time. I think it's important to know yourself before beginning a life together with another person. This doesn't mean others who get married younger are wrong. It just means it has worked differently for me. I see life as a series of phases, and marriage comes after the business phase, for me. I feel with the odds against a successful marriage so high in my line of work, I'll be better prepared for it if I have a stable life with financial security. This will enable me to have more family time instead of being forced to play half the year and juggle a family at the same time. For me, marriage and football do not go well together.

Third Time's the Charm

There are women that have gotten away; more specifically, there have been two that have caused some regrets. The first lady I met during my youthful fun stage. She was the only one that I would want to stay home with instead of being out all night with the homeboys on South Beach. I miss those relaxing nights in Miami with her. I will never forget the day that we met at the Miami Fair. I saw her standing on a small hill. The air itself had a special feel to it—the cotton candy, the funnel cakes, all the rides; everything, including her, combined into such a sweet atmosphere. Things slowed down when I was with her. She was my dream girl, but I didn't have the right balance at the time. I miss what we had; it was a deep connection. Her smile, her skin, her lips. I loved talking to her, whether it was face to face or over the phone. However, it wasn't meant to be. The combination of my new money ways and family issues confused me. I was so focused on trying to get myself together that once we broke up, the road to recovery couldn't happen fast enough for us.

I met the second love of my life more recently, just as I turned my attention to business. We started off as friends. In fact, I never thought I would fall for her. She was in an on-and-off relationship with another guy, and I was focused on getting my financial life in order; yet I was still drawn to her. I really liked that she was business savvy, educated, and street smart. Time flew by when we were together, and we could talk for hours about anything. I loved when she called me P.B. I can still hear it: "P.B., I need you." I tried to play it cool, but her eyes, lips, skin, and body mesmerized me. Her unexpected visits hypnotized me. This was not supposed to happen, but she left a stain on my brain. I got jealous if I knew she was around that other guy. I wanted the best for her, even though it didn't include me. Two sharp minds belong together, but I wasn't willing to take my focus off business, so our relationship died a natural death.

I did not want to settle down early like many of my New Money Millionaire friends. I was too busy trying to figure things out, especially life after football. I'd become accustomed to a certain lifestyle, having nice things. I wanted to get to the point where when I bring another person into my life, whether it is a wife or a child, it happens smoothly—without it affecting the comfortable lifestyle to which I am accustomed.

I'm still waiting for that one woman to walk into my life that will make it seem as if time is frozen. Her past does not matter to me. I want a woman who is with me and respects my space and knows what makes me I tick. She will demand my attention to a certain degree but support my efforts to achieve my goals. Ideally, she would be an established woman that is used to success. When that type of love comes, I'm all for it. For me, I'm looking for an overachiever, not just a sexy diva. And so the saying goes, "The third time is the charm." I hope.

For now, it's all about being patient and working towards my goals. The thought of starting a new family and pursuing such a strenuous professional goal at the same time is extremely overwhelming. I could not imagine dealing with the pressure from my immediate family, the need to work hard on the field, and the idea of starting a new family. I'm not that kind of multitasker. The balancing act requires time and dedication, and I want to be completely committed to each. If I juggled both a wife and football, I knew one would have to be sacrificed eventually. Just as I felt it easier to cope with one credit card instead of four, I find it easier to deal with one phase of life and then the next.

We all have the families we are born into that force us into making decisions that make us feel selfish. But add to this a new family and a high-stress, high-risk NFL career, not to mention all the money, and the pot starts to boil just a little bit hotter and faster. I've noticed other New Money Millionaires are often put in a position of having to choose between their blood family and the new one they are trying to start. This is a recipe for disaster. I have trust issues and apprehensions—baggage I need to work out—regarding my own family before I jump into a new one.

Being the Father You Never Had

As a New Money Millionaire, I knew I did not want to have kids while playing a sport. If you're a father while you're in the game, this means for every year in the league you miss out on more than half a year your child is alive. If you had a child the first year you're in the league and they're ten years old by the time you retire, you were present for less than five years of your child's life. I wonder if anyone ever thinks about it like this. It's one less month, one less week and even one less minute you have to be a positive influence, to ensure that your son or daughter grows up to be the man or woman that you want him or her to be. You will miss ballet lessons, school performances, and willl not get to know their friends. I want to be a role model for my kids because that is something that I never had as a child. When your child is eighteen or so (maybe even earlier), they're gone. Mentally checked out. Their relationship with their parents is different from that point onward.

When I growing up my father was not really around. When I was a young boy I constantly heard stuff about my father not claiming me. The craziest thing about it was that I didn't have a traditional absent dad, like a lot of kids who grow up in single-parent households. I saw my father in passing. When we interacted, he treated me just like any other kid, probably because he was my teacher and my coach.

I ended up in my father's English class when I was in seventh grade. When I made the middle school basketball team in the eighth grade my dad was the head coach. I always wanted him to pull me aside and teach me lessons, one-on-one. That never happened, and it was a little disappointing because I kept hearing about how good he was at basketball.

When I finally summoned the courage to ask why he never was around when I was a boy, he told me it was because his dad did the same thing to him. That was a surprise. You would think that he would want to do the opposite—give his son the time and attention he never received. I never understood his logic. When the money came, he suddenly wanted to play dad. The relationship between him and I felt forced, and I didn't think it could ever become normal.

Children bring difficult financial obligations. The problems get worse if you are unmarried and paying child support. Unfortunately, this happens to a lot of professional athletes. It becomes an eighteen-year problem, not because of the kid but because of the potential baby-mama drama and financial toll. There is nothing wrong with being a single dad, or an unmarried father, if you understand your obligations and you make an effort to fulfill them. If you are a responsible adult, it is an eighteen-year mortgage, with escalating payments. While I cannot speak from personal experience, I have close friends on both the male and female side of this. If it doesn't work out, it gets expensive. As soon as lawyers get involved, it affects the parent-child relationship in a negative way. More often than not, it is the father-child relationship that suffers most.

One day, I was sitting in the barbershop and the guy getting a haircut next to me was talking about a conversation he had with his son. The guy was threatening to change his number if his son gave it out to his mother or anybody else. He told his son, "If I give you my number and you give it to your mother or somebody else, then I'm changing my number and you and me will only communicate through social networks." While he had us all laughing at the thought of him changing his number and only speaking to his son through Facebook or Twitter, his point was profound, and I did not overlook it. Beyond the immediate comedy, this was a sad scene. This guy wanted to make it clear to his son that his relationship was with him alone, not him and his mother. I'm sure this is not an isolated family dynamic. It likely occurs in all families and in all walks of life.

Apart from the drama of having a child outside of marriage, there is also a selfish element to my decision to hold off on children.

Regardless of whether you are a professional athlete or a businessman in pursuit of your dream, having a child, especially out of wedlock, can significantly alter the time and energy you have to dedicate to your ultimate goals. When I have kids, I want to be able to spend time with them and have the money to send them to the best schools and colleges; I want to give them all the opportunities that are available and the best life I possibly can.

Different Stages for Different Ages

As I mentioned before, I see life as a series of stages: the having fun stage, the business stage, the getting myself completely together stage, and then the marriage and family stage. My current stage usually drives my actions. As I write this book, I am in the business stage of my life. Youth is over, and the beginning of middle age is looming around the corner. I don't know how long this phase will take, but meeting the right woman might fast-forward me a bit, moving me more quickly toward marriage. You can never say never when it comes to matters of the heart, and matters of the heart do not often follow your personal timetable.

Similarly, I might like a woman, but find her to be slowing me down or taking me backwards. At that point, she is a distraction. I've seen a lot of guys build their lives around talking to women every day on the phone, in person, or through endless texts. It is all about the ladies, 24/7. To me, their objective is to raise their girl count, not their net worth or personal account. When you begin multiplying the girl count, you end up dividing your time and energy, eventually depleting your bank account.

The balancing act of life has its strange twists and turns and its endless ironies and contradictions. Why is it that some of these guys can manage a half dozen or more women at once, but they can't manage two credit cards, a couple of homes and cars, or their personal lives? If they devoted more time to managing themselves, they could perhaps accomplish great things in the business world.

Let's Talk About Sex

Most of you who are reading this have probably sat through sex education classes in school, but I feel obligated to repeat the basics. Why? Because when you have money and there are attractive women around you all the time, you forget what it was all about. It's funny when a guy says, "A girl tricked me" or, "I was set up." There certainly are girls out that are Oscar-worthy: they are actors putting on a show. I call them feel-good girls. They have a way of making you feel good, telling you what you want to hear and feeding your ego. As it pertains to sex, the key line is, "I'm on the pill." That's great, but I don't want to hear all that. A guy knows every time you have sex without a condom, the chance of getting a girl pregnant goes up significantly. Let's say you go ahead and have sex without a condom or you do use a condom but it breaks. In today's day and age, you still have options to address the situation.

I'm not a shill for Planned Parenthood, but I don't want to hear your lame excuse: "I didn't know." You damn sure did. You learned that in fifth grade and, if you didn't, you saw it in a movie. There are no excuses. If you can't manage yourself or make decisions with the mindset of *would I be okay having a child with this woman?* then you better wear a condom or expect the emotional and financial responsibility that goes along with an unplanned pregnancy. Think before you act.

Shady Ladies

After unsuccessful nights of trying to come up with a way to understand women in my life, I decided to change the scenery and head back to Ft. Myers. I had plans to meet up with a lady, and she ended up inviting me over to her place. Time got away from me, and before I knew it, I was so tired I found myself half-asleep. She told me that I could stay over and invited me to sleep in her bed so I wouldn't have to sleep on the couch. Usually, I do not sleep over a girl's house—this is a golden rule of mine. But this time, it slipped away from me.

You know when you're coming out of sleep and you're not sure if the conversation you are hearing is happening in your dream or really happening? Well, the next morning as I was slowly waking up, I thought I was dreaming, and in my dreams, I was overhearing a conversation:

"Why are you at my place?"

"Don't act brand new. I've been over here," a male voice said.

But then I heard that same voice at a much closer distance. "What are you doing here?" he asked. When I opened my eyes, there was a big black guy, with that prison top-heavy stature, standing over me. "What are you doing here?" he repeated. But he didn't wait for my answer. "This is my girl," he said. We were in a situation where I wanted to say right away, "It's not what you think." But you've seen that in dozens of awkward movie scenes and magazine cartoons.

I was thinking, *this is your girl?* Why the hell was I in her bed? I didn't even ask to sleep there. He went on, interrogating me: "Did you have sex?" I said, "No, we did not have sex." We were just friends, I added.

"Are you Buchanon?" he asked.

Great, I thought to myself, *I just slept in the same bed as his girlfriend, and he knows who I am.* I reverted to the movies and cartoons: "Look, it ain't what you think it is. I'm going to get up out of here because it's a total misunderstanding."

Remember how I said I never do this? This is exactly why. I broke my own rule: With casual relationships, always play home games, never away games. Make the woman come to you. I was mad at myself. I didn't know her situation, and that was my mistake, not hers. I could have gotten hurt or killed by this Situation Woman.

Situation Woman [si-chə-wā-shən wûmən] ▶ *n.*

1. A female that is about your situation and not you; focused on what you have and not who you are.
2. She does not love you but loves what you can offer.
3. Typically involves an ulterior motive and hidden agenda, short-term or long-term (i.e., baby mama).
4. Her acting skills are Academy Award material; she makes you feel good and tells you what you want to hear.
5. Dependent, not independent.
6. Views you as synonymous to a winning lottery ticket and is ready to cash in—before she cashes out (i.e., after a divorce).
7. Could be a Historical Friend, Fun Friend, or a form of a Financial Molester.

Call me somewhere between cautious and paranoid, but when you are with a woman like I was, you have to ask yourself the most important question: *Was she there for me—or my situation, stature, and money?* I did something out of the norm to appease my boredom and found myself in a place where she could have set me up to get robbed by her boyfriend. I still think I was set up, used even. If this girl were genuine, she would not have put me in that predicament. The way I see it—and maybe I am paranoid, but I've seen this enough to know better—this could have been a call for her boyfriend to step up to the plate, seeing that a guy, an NFL player at that, was chilling with his girl. I, after all, offered to stay on the couch, she insisted on me staying in the bed and hours later I had an angry black man waking me from my sleep. Not a good outcome.

With this incident came many other memories where girls weren't about me, they were about where I stood in the food chain of status and resources. Another story that comes to mind involved a friend, his girl, and I. I knew he was seeing a woman that really liked him. She told him she wanted to have a baby with him.

He said to me one day, "I'm going to go chill with Keysha."
I laughed.

"Why you laughing?" he asked, confused.

"Nothing, it's just funny that we're talking to girls with the same name," I said, not realizing things were about to get even more confusing.

"Wait, what does your Keysha look like?" my friend asked.

Well, I'll be damned; we were both interested in the same girl. She was keeping us both on the hook to see who was going to get reeled in first. I think her best friend was an accomplice because she would tell me how much Keysha was into me. She definitely didn't realize how close this other guy and I were. This was yet another fortune hunter.

I soon began to realize and accept the fact that this trend wasn't going to stop until my bank account dropped. I didn't want my bank account to dwindle, so I had to learn the difficult lesson of reading the signs of a Situation Female.

Here is another weird story about this kind of woman. When I lived in Houston, while playing for the Texans, I started talking to a girl. One thing led to another, and we eventually had sex. We continued to have sex. This went on for about a month. One day I was pulling into my driveway with one of my boys, Andre, when my phone rang, "Hello," I answered. It was the girl I was talking to.

"Hello . . . hold on a minute."

"Hey, man, I just have a question," came a voice from the other side of the line. And it wasn't a girl's voice, that was for sure, and definitely not the voice I had been sleeping with for the past month. "This is my girl you've been talking to. I want to know if you've been having sex with her," the voice continued.

What? I thought to myself. *Wait a minute, she calls me, says hello, and puts her boyfriend on the phone? I'm confused.*

The man went on, "I just want to let you know I'm a big fan of yours. I follow you."

This was crazy to me that I had no idea what this dude looked like, but he knew what I looked like. I don't know if he threw in the fact he was a fan so I'd be more candid with him or what. He continued, "I really love her, and I would kill someone over her." When I heard that, I was thinking, *Damn, this man is really serious.* I pictured myself going to restaurants like the Breakfast Club, Blacksmith, or a local place in Houston, and this dude coming up and sitting down at the table next to me, and I'd have no idea who it was, and bam . . . my life would be over.

I'm no idiot, though. I told him, "Man, look, I didn't mess with your girl. Sorry for the misunderstanding," and then I quickly hung up the phone. That was a lie, of course, but a lie of survival. In philosophy, utilitarians believe that lying is only wrong if it causes more pain than pleasure. The way I saw it, if I told him we had sex, many times, she was going to cry, he was going to get mad, and I was going to be dead. Not a good outcome. I know utilitarians would have my back on that one. No way was I wrong for lying in that situation. I averted a hostile reaction and a violent episode.

Love and lust will follow new money and the pro athlete around every corner. Drum that sentence into your head. Unless you want to live a totally sheltered, monkish existence, you will need to learn how to look around those corners. Try to think with your brain, and don't react and make hasty decisions because you are being coerced with activity that occurs below your waist.

Understand what the give and take is in every new relationship. If you don't, you will end up making bad decisions that can heap huge consequences on your life.

Chapter 9

Training for Life

You Trained Your Whole Life, So Don't Stop Now

From a very young age, a person embarks on a lifelong journey of training. For many, that means training through twelve years of education to get in a position to pursue higher education. I trained because I was hungry to get to the NFL. But preparation comes in different forms and is not always referred to as training. Think about your own training. You may be a new artist with a hit record, a young actor who just got a big break, a young internet entrepreneur who became a newly minted millionaire, or a businessman in the professional world who just struck it rich after a long dig.

But then what? What happens after you reach your professional dream? What happens when you decide to redefine what success means to you—head in a different direction—whether because you want to or have no choice to break from the professional world? Training does not end even if you retire early from your first profession. You must retrain your mind for your next achievement or life pursuit and ignite your Postgame.

Postgame [pōst-gām]*n.*
1. The realization that one career has ended and new ones will open as new talents and skills evolve.
2. Results in a win or loss (i.e., buying a new house or moving back into your mother's house).

3. Transitioning to a lifestyle that will continue to grow your money.
4. Developing a game plan to win in the next chapter of life.

Preparing financially for life is no different from preparing for a game; you have to put in the workout time. But while in sports the old cliché of "no pain, no gain" is true, in the financial world the ultimate goal is "much gain, with little to no pain." If you don't work out your brain in the financial game, however, you are bound to end up burned—no financial gain, and a lot of pain.

Training Phases—An Overview

The training that goes on over the course of one's life can be broken into three phases: pre-training, training, and post-training. As you progress through the three phases, the control shifts. You progress from others telling you what to do, to you determining your every move. In other words, you go from being a mentee, being able to stand on your own two feet, to one day being able to become a mentor yourself.

In the pre-training phase, your life is more structured and the least flexible simply because you may not know any better and others are leading the way. These people are like your training wheels. The pre-training phase takes you through high school, and for those who are fortunate enough, college too. For me, it was my Uncle Curtis and then my other uncle after Uncle Curtis died. Then it was my mother and my grandmother that provided the structure. Your pre-training is what gets you to your training phase. My training phase came in the NFL—this too had a mold, a structure, a system I had to follow. I had to buy into the organization I was playing for. If I didn't, I no longer had a place there.

It isn't until the post-training phase that you have complete control. For me, it was the most exciting, but for those without any pre-training, it can be the scariest.

Pre-training

Your pre-training started many years ago while you were in elementary school. From day one, you were taught hard work and repetition in order to accomplish your goals. Pre-training—all kinds, in fact— requires mental concentration toward a combination of fitness and physical work.

You followed your teacher's rules and memorized the multiplication tables so you could perform well on a math exam. And, like many people who complain about required courses in school, you probably wondered why you needed to know the multiplication tables. You disciplined yourself to be at an appointment at least five minutes early—remembering that to be early is to be on time and to be on time is to be late. If you started sports early, you were taught to train in practice so you can be prepared to compete.

You learned manners—or at least I hope you did. You were trained to hold the door open and let others walk in before you because you watched your father do it growing up. Your mother trained you how to act civilly in public, not to scream in the grocery store. At dinner, you were told not to put your elbows on the table. Some of your training had cultural and humorous aspects, as well. You were trained not to ask a pregnant woman when she was due, how old she was, and to hedge the question or outright tell a white lie when she asks you whether a dress she is wearing makes her look fat. Gender diplomacy, yes, was part of your training.

Your approach to pre-training is largely determined by your will and desire. A positive attitude is the prerequisite to all kinds of discipline and training. For me, will and desire came naturally. In high school, I went out late at night running, practicing, putting in extra hours. When training at odd hours, my motivation was knowing that I was working while my opponent is out partying, sleeping, or doing something other than working out. It gives you the mental edge because you're putting in more hours.

I used that time for visualizing the plays I would make Friday night under the lights. Sometimes it would be 1:00 or 2:00 in the morning on a school night, but this was a part of my training plan. On weekends, when everyone was out partying, I was training to get better. For me, training didn't stop when practice ended. For others, they depended solely on practice structure to guide them each step of the way.

Regular practice, however, is not enough if you want to someday become an elite athlete. I went a little beyond the structure provided and added extra hours. If you pay attention to your training, you learn from it; it helps you develop good habits. Bad training leads to bad habits. Right now, this is an ongoing debate in education when it comes to tracking students. Placing a kid on an honors track is providing a training that is rigorous compared to a student placed on a remedial track or even a general track. The honors student gets to compete with the best in the classroom, and often the expectations placed on those students are higher. Maybe your training didn't look like mine; regardless, in your own training, you are put through a series of drills until certain behaviors become habit. (See Malcolm Gladwell's best-selling book of 2008, *Outliers*. He constantly points to a generally recognized fact that it takes 10,000 hours of practical instruction, training, and practice to become an expert at anything. This will make you think twice when you read about someone in any endeavor who suddenly becomes an "overnight sensation." It does not work that way. He or she has been at it for 10,000 hours or more. And this doesn't necessarily mean you'll make the grade. It just means you will likely get to a level of general excellence.).

While pre-training comes with structure, it can also lead to a false sense of believing you can't fail. This is different from a general "positive attitude." Looking back, I see that the structure was provided to me as a student-athlete in college was merely a pair of crutches. When it came time to entering the real world, college had crippled me. As a student-athlete, there were systems in place—certain safety nets—to catch me before I fell. Whether it was mandatory study hall the first two semesters to make sure I transitioned well from high school, or being given the number of a police officer to call to minimize the publicity if I ever got in trouble.

I was told when to wake up, when to eat, when to go to class, when to work out, when to be at practice, and when to go to bed. This kind of structure is not quite military discipline, but it is discipline. These systems made it very difficult for me to fall off the grid. That said, when it was time to move on to the next phase in my life, I understood that the structure was bound to change as well. Since you will be supervising much of your own training, you cannot assume that the same safeguards will be in place to protect you from failure when you reach professional status and move into the next training phase.

Training

Your pre-training phase puts you in place to become a professional, whether you become a CEO of a Fortune 500 company, a professional athlete, or a high-level lawyer. For me, it was the NFL. Your professional status triggers a phase where you must maintain a level of training that will enable you to continue your success at that level. Just climbing that first mountain is not enough. There are others to conquer, and as soon as you lose sight of this you have unconsciously given up on your goals.

This applies to personal achievements as well. If you trained hard in the gym and counted calories to get yourself to a target weight, your eating habits shouldn't go backward once you've achieved that weight. It is a matter of maintenance and training habits (This is why the nutrition industry uses the terms "yo-yo diet" and "diets don't work." They apply to people who just add the weight back again after they lose it. It's a constant personal battle. All it really means is discipline and training started and then stopped.).

You already know what you need to do to maintain a certain degree of success. While you no longer need the direction of others to train you, this phase is still very much about fitting into a mold that someone else has created—a mold that meets the needs and expectations of a supervisor, customer, or coach. Think about it, even if you own your own company, you have consumers that need to be satisfied if you expect them to continue investing in your service or product (Everyone has a boss—even the CEO of a large public company. In fact, he has several bosses; they're called the board of directors.).

Essentially, you are told how to act, what to wear, when to show up, when to leave, how to sign your emails, what you can and cannot ask a prospective employee if you are in a hiring position . . . the list goes on. The training template is transferable to a certain degree to a number of different jobs or assignments.

For me, there were certainly behavioral expectations and a schedule to follow. A typical day in the NFL started with a meeting at around 8:00 in the morning. A typical team meeting lasted about twenty to thirty minutes, depending on the previous win or loss. After the team meeting, we split into offense and defense meetings. I would head out with the rest of the defense to our designated meeting room, where we made corrections from previous errors or implemented new plays for an upcoming game as a whole defensive unit.

In the business world, middle-level executives constantly complain about too many meetings, meetings that end with scheduling more meetings. Meetings where there are too many people to make any headway on a given issue. In fact, a business mantra has long been, "There are just too many meetings."

But meetings are critical in one respect. When people speak, they reveal aspects of their character. The person who called and is running the meeting usually does the most talking. That tells a lot, as well. The degree to which you fit the team mold and obey orders determines how personal it will get in meetings. I remember sitting in one defense meeting, and a coach said, "We've got a player with his dick in his hands that thinks he knows everything." I knew he was talking about me. The coach never said my name, but I knew he was talking about me because I did sit in the back with my hands in my pants to keep warm, because I was always freezing (The coaches keep the meeting rooms cold intentionally so no one falls asleep).

Other coaches would embarrass a player by name if he wasn't fitting the team mold. This happened to me only once during a defense meeting for not reaching the coach's expectations in the previous game. He claimed that I didn't like to tackle. To humiliate me, he had me go outside and hit the popsicle (the name given for a dummy bag). There are more ways than one to motivate players. Broadly, we're talking about "positive" reinforcement or "negative" reinforcement. This coach used the negative. Some leaders think this works (General George Patton is the most famous military man who comes to mind. He thought nothing of slapping a soldier who was in a hospital for stress disorder.).

Not all coaches use negative training tactics, of course. When I played for University of Miami coach Butch Davis, he always tried to give us life pointers during meetings and give players the opportunity to shine. One particular time it backfired. During a team meeting, he was breaking down his money expenditures on a pie chart: "My wife gets a slice, my kids get a slice . . ." Next he called on one of the veteran players, thinking he would set a good example. "So how would you divide your pie?" Davis asked. The player stood up and said, "A slice to my mom, each of my cousins, my girl, my old coach, my . . ." The coach cut him off, saying, "Ah, fuck, you have too many slices in your pie. You're going to be broke." It was a funny moment with a lot of truth behind it. That said, be prepared for whatever the meeting may bring, both the good and the bad.

In the NFL, there's really no picking and choosing what part of their system you want to buy into and what part you don't. This includes even little things, like the food they serve you for lunch. I expected the NFL food to be good, given the amount of money they were paying us, but it was unusually awful. You might as well have been eating airline food. It's sad that most days I settled for a peanut butter and jelly sandwich. In my third year with the Raiders, I brought up the food situation with our general manager. After listening quietly to my complaint, he said, "Get your ass down on that football field and worry about how to get better, not the food we are feeding you." I learned to eat the food or go hungry. Was the subpar food an intentional motivational tool? It's not worth analyzing.

Every organization has different rules and expectations. The dress code, for example, varies widely. One team I played for expected that you went to meetings dressed ready to go out on the field. The clubhouse personnel had your equipment organized so you only had to pick it up on your way out. There was no looking around for a pad here or getting new gloves. Other teams expected you to do this yourself.

Some teams taught you the hard way if you weren't prepared. You'd get a letter in your locker with a notice of a $250 or $500 fine for being late on the field. I was once fined for using the bathroom during a meeting, for being on the toilet too long. I think you see this more when you play for losing organizations. When the coaching sucks and your losses far outnumber your wins, they do anything to make it difficult on the players. In their minds, they feel they tried the nice-guy approach, and it didn't work. So rather than refine their strategy, they just say, "We'll do a 180-degree turn and treat the players like dogs."

Regardless of how you view this, it's a training tactic. You either hold in your bodily fluids to meet their expectations or you break a rule and suffer the consequences. When the fines start piling up, you will start having your pads already loosened, ready to throw on, or visiting the men's room on your lunch break.

After an hour and a half to two hours of formal practice, there was, at times, another meeting to go over film from practice. Some guys would come in smelly to the meeting, and others would spare us and shower first. I knew that I learned best from watching film. I tried to finish lunch early so I would have time to go in and watch more film. The more film I watched, the more the plays talked to me on the field. Again, repetition is a training technique.

Training isn't always easy (generally speaking, it's not supposed to be that much fun), especially if you are paid by a losing organization. In the best-case scenario, there are systems in place to help you learn what it takes to fit their mold, but even then, this does not guarantee success. Some people can't cope with certain criteria. This is true for me with a few teams I played for. One coach in the NFL didn't allow the cornerbacks to speak to the rest of the defense on the field during the game. I did not understand the logic behind this and had a hard time coping with it. Part of me still thinks I should have continued to do what I knew would bring out the best in me on the field, but it wasn't what that particular organization wanted.

This is a hard life lesson to absorb: I learned that once you study with excellent teachers, it is hard to cope with anyone that's less than excellent. Good coaches set a high standard. At the beginning of my career, I found myself in a tough situation. I was young in the league, and I wasn't happy. I didn't play my best. Failure during training can result from two things: you are part of a bad system in which you are unable to cope, or you simply think you know it all. If you're not willing to conform to a certain norm, there comes a point where you find yourself forced to part ways. For me, it was a new contract with a different NFL team. For you, it may mean interviewing for a new position.

Post-training

Post-training is equivalent to self-training. In this phase, you are in complete control. Your complete success and failure begins and ends with you. You can trace life's victories and defeats to many causes, but in the end, you're in the driver's seat. Moving from the training phase to the post-training phase is the most difficult task you'll face. It is here where you put your Postgame plan into play.

This transition is one that must occur gradually. It is not as if the training phase ends one day and you wake up the next day in your post-training phase. It is an inevitable phase, and you should begin preparing for it sooner than you think. For this reason, it's important to have a Postgame plan sketched out in advance. Most people stop at the training phase, so when it is time to make the transition, they have no idea what to do or where to begin. A dwindling bank balance usually prompts the decision. They find that their financial stability is crumbling under their feet, and they are not sure what direction will lead them to solid ground.

On the one hand, this phase is scary, but on the other, post-training is the most exciting. It is during this phase that you have almost total ownership. In my case, financially, I was handed a lot of money almost overnight. I eventually came to see that money as Head-Start Money, but that took a while. It took a great deal of pre-training and training to come to understandings about how best to put my money to good use.

The time that elapses for each person, in each of his training phases, will vary. I knew that the average NFL career was less than three years. So I learned to start preparing for my Postgame early. I did not want to become another statistic in the "average" category, so I started post-training earlier than most.

First, I took advantage of an offering from the NFL called the Business Management and Entrepreneurship Program, which aims to improve NFL players' business skills and helps their ability to evaluate business opportunities. I had an opportunity to enroll in workshops at the Harvard Business School, the Kellogg School of Management (Northwestern University), and the Wharton School of the University of Pennsylvania. This was the start of my transition, even though my NFL career has not yet ended. Attending these classes was one way to stay hungry and put myself in a place to live without financial stress, a long-term plan.

The post-training phase is critical for anyone who is in a situation like mine: someone who found success early and has been able to maintain that success but is currently undergoing a change in lifestyle. Because of the NFL-sponsored opportunities and workshops I took advantage of, my life did not require radical reform.

I am still learning to adapt to something new. I had to go on a financial diet. I spend less and invest more. This is all part of my Postgame plan. I am slowing down, regrouping. I'm taking the time to develop a new game plan so I can win in the next chapter of my life. I feel that I maximized the financial opportunity I was given as an NFL player, but now it is equally important for me to adapt and adjust my mind-set to ease the transition into a lifestyle that will continue to grow my money without the support of the NFL. I want to do all this and better myself. Both are essential and involve a degree of balancing.

One of those balancing acts involves how much you surround yourself with the right people, and how much solitude—strictly "me" time—you allot for yourself. A lot of people like having a support structure around them all the time, an entourage. This is not always the wisest way to go (Think of Mike Tyson, who never traveled light as a heavyweight champion. But after a spectacular downfall, he's become a regular family guy and the entourage has long disappeared from his life. His Fun Friends are in his distant past.).

I can't stress enough the importance of taking time for independent reflection; this is crucial to transition and growth. Growth is what happens when you spend time alone dreaming, reflecting, and planning. This alone time allows you to sort your thoughts, establish your priorities, set short and long-term goals, and formulate a plan of action. Thinking alone, does not mean acting alone. You act with people that are on the same page as you, looking to maximize their success and ultimately better their lives.

Show Me Your Friends, I'll Show You Your Future

I mentioned in a previous chapter that the top five friends in a person's life, the five people you hang out with the most tells you a lot about a person. Your friends reveal your true character. The people you surround yourself with on a daily basis are the people that influence you most. Poor company corrupts good character. When you're around bad people long enough, your own character is jeopardized. If your closest friends are connected to drugs, it's likely that you may get caught up in drugs, directly or peripherally. Maybe you tell yourself that you're just helping your friend out, giving him some extra cash when he needs it, but soon his habit becomes your problem; you become his go-to money lender, and you start losing control of the reins you thought you were holding on to so tightly. By the time you realize what he's using your borrowed money for, it's too late. Generosity is not a bad thing; you just need to know whom you are helping out and why you are helping them out (I've covered this in detail earlier, but this is a good place to remind you once again. The company you keep will determine how you deal with any given phase of your life, and your path to growing.).

Your friends play a role in your ultimate success, so choose them wisely. They are an active part of your training process, whether they know it or not. Some friends are wise, others are simply there when you need them, but these are the people that will help you rise. Take a good look around you and ask yourself whether the people closest to you are working with you or against you.

Some Friends Uplift, Some Push You Off the Cliff

I find that my top five friends have changed as I've gone from one phase to the next. When I was young, it was Marvin, Kevin, Fred, Nick, and Steve. Marvin was my first friend; we were from the same hood. We were both good at sports from day one—football, basketball, and track. Kevin was the cleanest guy I knew and still is to this day. He stayed next door to Marvin's grandmother's house. He was the guy who brought his own blanket and pillow to sleepovers. He was a lady's man in high school; he always wore fresh outfits, nice shoes, and sported a fresh haircut at all times. Hell, he only ate fresh food. You could eat three meals and a snack at Kevin's crib. It was almost like being at a college dining hall; you even had a large menu.

Fred was the smartest kid in my crew at the time. He was the only guy I actually saw get help on his homework from his mother. This should tell you about the kind of parenting we had to endure in the hood. The rest of us were on our own. Fred's refrigerator looked like Walmart to me; it never ran out of food. His mother would cook for us all the time. That breakfast smelled so good in the morning it would wake me up from my sleep on his bedroom floor. Nick was the most genuine and loyal friend I had ever met at that time. He and his dad took me in as a family member when I moved out of my mother's house in high school. All of our teammates and guys could hang out at Nick's house because his dad was cool.

We had movie nights with girls, and we would egg cars together—normal neighborhood kid's stuff. We'd make our Walmart runs for chicken fingers, stuffing two bags of chicken fingers into one. Lastly, there was Steve—the jokester of the crew, and a self-proclaimed rapper. Anytime he got a chance, he would test his skills either in a studio or just recording himself on tape. Steve and Marvin were part of a rap group while we were in middle school. I remember staying up late at night talking to girls with Steve. He would change his voice to sound just like a girl when he called over to their house;

this avoided conflict with any of the girls' dads. It worked every time, and he even taught me how to do it. We got so good at changing our voices that we would prank call each other to see how far the conversation would go before either of us figured out it was a joke. Steve prank called me a lot more than I prank called him. Anyway, these were the guys that were around for pre-training.

When I transitioned into my training phase, Nick was still a part of that top five, but he'd gone off to college and moved in with his girlfriend. Then there were the two Andre's, Clint, and Banks. The first Andre came into the picture around the time of my first national championship at Miami. He is Nick's younger brother, so we talked a lot while I was in college. He was a little bit more sensitive than I was, very organized and creative. Sometimes he would turn into Frank the Tank, but it was all fun and games.

The other Andre was a teammate who I could relate to. We were always on the same page about pretty much everything. We had similar personalities and were highly motivated, determined to make things happen. I respected him because he respected everyone. He was also laid back like myself; together we were too cool for school.

Clint was my roommate and the ultimate entertainer when it came to girls, showing off and joking. His mother also spoiled him. When he needed to wash his clothing, he would immediately send them out to mom and receive them back to campus within two to three days ironed and pressed like they came from the cleaners. Plus, there was a bonus package of soul food and snacks (I really appreciated Clint's mom, because I was eating some of that soul food myself; I can still taste it.). I had no choice but to wash my own clothing. There was no way my mother would do for me what Clint's mother did for him. My clothing went missing in high school or got bleached-out in the wrong places. When it came to girls, no one did it better; at least that's what he would say.

Banks was someone I met through my agent, and I viewed him as a man who knew more than me and kept me grounded. He knew every trick in the bag to get a girl; he was very hip to the game. He may even have topped Clint as the perfect entertainer when it came to telling stories and girls. I used to beat him so badly in the video game NFL Fever, like 50–7, that he started staying up all night to practice while I was sleeping. He tried so hard to figure out my tricks, but they never worked. I would walk out of my room around 3:00 AM to get a snack from the refrigerator, and he would act like he was asleep. I knew he wasn't because I had just heard him talking to the video game. I purposely took a long time so that he would get a delay-of-game penalty. I heard him from the hall once; he said, "Man this punk done messed me up. Now it's third-and-25, dang." I admit that got me laughing.

Now that I have reached my post-training phase, my top five are different guys, but they play an integral role in my life. It is this phase that I am the most vulnerable, because the mold has been lifted. I get to create my own template, and for this reason, those that hold influence around me are of utter importance.

First there's Nate. I know Nate from college, through Clint. He's a hard worker and a very goal-driven Jewish kid. He went on to law school and became an attorney. Despite his success, he has remained grounded, which is one of the things I really love about the guy. He's also loyal, respectful, and loves to work out as much as he loves to eat (If you love to eat, you have to work out.). He finishes his plates faster than me and is always up for eating something anytime.

Next, there is Junior. He serves as my spiritual advisor. We can talk about football and track all day long, at any level—high school, college, or professional. He is an educator, a hard worker, and a fast learner. I admire his ability to grasp things quickly. I also respect that he is proudly and happily married.

Then there's Darien, who I met when I went back to school at Miami. He is now attending law school at NYU, about to become a lawyer, just like Nate. He's not only been a huge part of my academic support system, but he also has a business mind so we bounce ideas off each other all the time. I can always count on him for a sound second opinion. His parents raised him the right way. When I heard that they offered him ten or twenty-dollar incentives to read a book and write a report on it, I was amazed. I love that his parents were so involved in his education from a very young age.

Then there's Lonnie. Lonnie is someone I met out in Los Angeles at Eve's TV show in 2003. Lonnie is really connected. He is an award winning writer and singer. He has introduced me to stars like Jamie Foxx, Beyoncé, Jay-Z, Meagan Good, and Kelly Rowland.

Last, there's Jonathan. He's the third lawyer of the group. He is also an astute businessman with a good spiritual balance. Though he started off as a mentor, over the years he has become a good friend. He is also like a big brother. He knows a lot of stuff and can evaluate a situation from a different perspective than I can, in a good way. Although we come from different backgrounds, we can relate to each other on multiple levels. When I mess up or do something out of the norm, he drops knowledge and wisdom on me.

To recap, know the difference among the three training phases of your life, and know that the last one never ends. Training is working, and working is learning, and the more you buy into this notion the better prepared you will be for life after your Head-Start Money. The last phase is the most difficult because you alone make the life-altering decisions. You need to listen, put all the advice you get from your respected inner circle into the blender, then take that first nervous sip on your own.

Chapter 10

From Failing to Acing:
Your Financial Intelligence Test

Your ability to navigate the early moments of your New Money Millionaire status is rooted in childhood. The type of structure a kid has growing up, and the people providing guidance along the way, sets a precedent for future behavior. That's why I admire Darien's parents so much. They prepared their son.

Most kids notice and react to the financial spending patterns they see growing up. If you grow up poor with no financial guidance, you have a tendency to buy the luxurious things you wished you could afford when you were a kid. It's only natural, until you see or learn something different. I grew up wearing the nicest shoes and nicest clothes. You might have guessed I came from an upper-middle-class neighborhood, but it was just that our priorities were all screwed up. As black kids from the hood, it was a sign of pride and self-esteem to have nice kicks.

As you get older, wiser, and grow in your financial intelligence, your thought processes change, as do your spending patterns and behaviors. The nature of New Money Millionaires is that they are not born into money. They aren't born rich or handed a guide that will get them through their New Money Millionaire phase successfully—a phase in which you are judged, evaluated, and even criticized by your peers, fans, and family. And, for this reason, it is a phase that not everyone comes into or out of equally equipped; yet everyone is graded on the same scale.

Consider the following four hypothetical scenarios after four high school students find $1,000 on the side of the street.

Student Number 1

The girl sees the money while walking down the street, and she calls her best friend and says, "Hey, girl, you won't believe what I just found."

"What?"

"I found a thousand dollars on the sidewalk."

"What are you going to do with it?"

"You already know I'm going to go get a pair of Christian Louboutins."

Student Number 2

He is equally surprised when he sees the money, and, he too, calls his best friend to tell him about his good fortune. But when his best friend asks, "What are you going to do with it?" all he says is, "I don't know."

After hanging up the phone, he thinks to himself, *I really don't know what to do, but I can use some nice things, and I know my momma has been complaining about the washing machine acting up.*

Student Number 3

This kid finds the money and doesn't bother with the phone. He immediately heads to his best friend's house to tell him about it. When he walks in the house, his best friend and best friend's father are sitting at the table. He says, "Man, guess what I just found."

"What?"

"A thousand dollars in cash on the side of the road."

"What are you going to do with it?"

"I don't know," the kid replies, and then turns to his friend's father. "Mr. Johnson, what do you think I should do with it?"

The father says, "I've got an idea. Why don't you go buy some used landscaping equipment? A lawnmower, Weed Wacker, an edger, whatever you can get for your money and start your own landscaping company. It'd be a good summer gig. Go around to the neighbors and offer to take care of their yard once a week, and set a fair price. I'll even be your first customer, and if you're good, I'll refer you to my buddies."

"Yeah, I like it."

"And if you get more people than you can handle, bring D.J. on board. He needs a summer job, anyway. He can help, and you can give him a cut of your earnings. You can end up making more than the thousand you started with."

Student Number 4

In the last scenario, the high middle school kid doesn't call his best friend. He goes home and tells his father, exclaiming that he's just become a thousandaire.

"Oh yeah, what do you mean by thousandaire?" the father asks.

"I found ten hundred-dollar bills on the side of the road."

"Okay, well let's think smart about this. I have a proposal. How about you take $500 to spend on what you'd like. You have to have some fun with your unexpected finding."

"What about the other half?"

"I propose you have me save it for you."

"Save it, why? That's no fun."

"How about if I told you that I would give it back to you at Christmas with 10 percent interest."

"Now you're talking."

Each student in the above scenarios grew up with a different kind of financial education, and yet, as I mentioned above, when they grow up their financial intelligence will be graded on the same level, on par with one another. Seems unfair, doesn't it? Which scenario do you think you would have followed had you been the one to find the money? Which one you chose will certainly reveal something about your financial character. But where you start isn't as important as where you're going and where you end up. The preceding scenes are about some of the options that are available.

Can You Pass the Test?

Let's imagine that you are enrolled in a class and are being graded. The good news is that you can grow and improve your score, just like in school. You can start out as a D student and become a B student. You can begin with a C and earn a B, too. But in order for you to earn an A in this environment, you must be born into a family (or adopted into one) that already has a wealth-management structure in place.

I imagine if New Money Millionaires were actually given a test, it would come with a clear set of instructions to know what it took to earn an A, B, C, D, or even F. It might look something like this:

You are reading these instructions because you are about to begin your New Money Millionaire test, which will occur exactly three years from today. You will be awarded a final grade of an A, B, C, D, or F based on where you stand at the end of this phase. The next few pages provide you with a grading scale, including detailed benchmarks that will be used to determine your final grade. Be sure to read through each definition twice, as there is an overlap in some indicators; however, pay close attention to the details that distinguish one grade from another.

You will find a sample budget following each definition that serves to emulate spending habits of a person in that grade range given $1 million to budget for one year. (Note: every person tested will be graded on an individual basis, and these budgets are only to serve as an example for a typical person that would earn that particular grade.)

Last, while your grade is transient throughout your time as a New Money Millionaire, your final grade rests solely on your rank exactly three years from the date you sign your first contract. Anything done after the specified deadline will not be considered in your final grade.

By turning the page, you are acknowledging that your time starts now, that you will read through the grading scale, definitions, and case studies thoroughly and you will try your best. Good Luck!

Are you an A, B, C, D?

Nobody starts with a failing grade. An A through D is what you are born into or what happens when you are a newborn millionaire, but an F is the result of what can happen. Prior to walking into any test, a student comes in with a set of skills, some stronger than others. Some stem from the family you are born into, the school you attend, the support you have around you, and the opportunities you are exposed to. Pretty much everyone has a unique background. Some will start with more smarts than others. Life is unfair, and understanding this at an early age is helpful. This is where a person has the choice to accept his or her situation or to "study" and improve his or her score.

Passing the New Money Millionaire test is no different. A person arrives at this point with a skill set; some useful ones they were fortunate enough to be born into, some they got with only a prayer, barely a vague idea what they're doing. Your position on the grading scale is transient until you fail. You've failed if you go bankrupt in less than three years.

Let me be clear, you can start at a C or D and study to grow and earn a B. I like to believe that no New Money Millionaire is handed money and given a blessing to fail. If you do nothing, expect to fail.

Also, your behavior and money-management skills will have a profound effect on the next generation. How you handle yourself as a parent will ultimately have consequences—both good and bad—on your children. Questions you should ask yourself are: Will you be instilling good money-handling habits in your kids? Are they around enough for you to have an influence on how they handle money? Or will you be leaving these lessons for your kids to learn on their own?

F is for Fuckup

F Person [eff pərsən] ▶ *n.*

1. Describes a person who is always right back where he/she started.

Instead of owning the club, buying your own table in VIP, or splitting a table with friends, or choosing to budget and settle for a few drinks at the bar, an F Person person is the bouncer. When you fail, you're stuck telling people to "get the F out" while Tina Turner's "Back Where You Started" is on replay in your head: "You'll be back where you started/I know how it feels when you've been discarded/Back where you started/You think you got it made but it won't get you far, no it won't get you far."

After looking at the worst outcome possible, let's navigate from A to D and try to avoid an F:

A *is for* Alpha Investor

A Person [Ay pərsən] ▶ *n.*

1. One who is born into a family with elite resources thanks to a history of successful businesses.
2. One who has a strong familial presence growing up which lays a strong foundation for his own decision-making.
3. One who strives to represent the family well, protects the family name in making decisions.
4. Can be known to spend smart, well versed in all loopholes and doesn't hesitate to write off bad investments before making them worse.
5. Can be found in a club charging his table to his father's credit card
6. One who equips himself with a game plan for marriage, children, and a stable future; likely to marry young to a

bombshell who will always look good by his side when the camera flashes.

Synonyms: Manning family (Archie, Peyton, and Eli), Rivers family (Doc and Austin), the Waltons (Jim, John, Alice, Rob, and Helen), any Kennedy family member, and the Simmons.

Sample Budget: The A Person			
Expenses	Amount	Balance	Notes
New Money	$ 1,000,000.00		
Taxes	$ 350,000.00	$ 650,000.00	Highest Tax Bracket
Rent	$ 30,000.00	$ 620,000.00	
Car(s)	$ 50,000.00	$ 570,000.00	Due to a family connection, paid nearly half the of ticket price
Investments	$ 400,000.00	$ 170,000.00	6-12% return rates
Food	$ 36,000.00	$ 134,000.00	
Travel	$ 15,000.00	$ 119,000.00	
Fun	$ 50,000.00	$ 69,000.00	
Legal Fees	?		Family covers cost
Mom Money	?		
Family Money	?		
Furniture	?		Family covers cost
CPA	?		Family covers cost
Fin. Advisor	?		Family covers cost
Misc.	$ 69,000.00	$ -	

B *is for* Beta Investor

B Person [Bee pərsən] ▶ *n.*

Often grows up in a lower-middle-class to poor family environment and depends on mentors who understand the value of money.

1. One who surrounds himself with well-educated, high-aspiring individuals.

2. Mentor(s) or family member(s) keeps spending habits in line but also knows when to enjoy himself (i.e., limited to one car that can meet his everyday functions and one car for fun).

3. Common for this person to make financial mistakes only with an amount of money he can afford to lose.

4. Can be found in a club with only the amount of money he budgets himself to spend (more often than not this means spending money on a few drinks, not a few bottles, if anything at all); however, will budget to go all out on special occasions.

5. Mindset is focused on the future (i.e., meeting his current needs modestly to enjoy wants down the road); in terms of girls, this typically means short-term, uncommitted relationships until he meets a woman that fits certain life qualifications.

Synonyms: Edgerrin James, Serena Williams, LeBron James, Beyoncé

Sample Budget: The B Person			
Expenses	Amount	Balance	Notes
New Money	$ 1,000,000.00		
Taxes	$ 350,000.00	$ 650,000.00	
Rent	$ 36,000.00	$ 614,000.00	
Car(s)	$ 110,000.00	$ 504,000.00	2 Cars
Investments	$ 300,000.00	$ 204,000.00	Money in an account to be moved after consulting with mentors
Food	$ 30,000.00	$ 174,000.00	
Travel	$ 25,000.00	$ 149,000.00	
Fun	$ 35,000.00	$ 114,000.00	
Legal Fees	$ 10,000.00	$ 104,000.00	Using a family member, friend, or referred lawyer
Mom Money	$ 59,000.00	$ 45,000.00	Includes loan money and house mortgage
Family Money	$ 25,000.00	$ 20,000.00	Emergency Fund
Furniture	$ 15,000.00	$ 5,000.00	
CPA	$ 4,000.00	$ 1,000.00	
Fin. Advisor	$ 1,000.00	$ -	
Misc.	?	?	

C *Is for* Confused Consumption

C Person [see pərsən] ▶ *n.*

1. Can be found pictured on the back of a milk carton for being lost along with the majority of other New Money

Millionaires; Is often lost for a few years during his career, which may lead to him being lost his entire career.

2. Relies only on his own counsel; often wrong, surrounded by Helium Mentors.

3. Known for rapid behavior changes that vary from modest to outrageous spending i.e., buying a table with friends and the next night buying his own table next to his friends.

4. Not uncommon to have a baby, baby mamma, get married, or all of the above.

Synonym: Phillip Buchanon as a New Money Millionaire

Sample Budget: The C Person			
Expenses	Amount	Balance	Notes
New Money	$ 1,000,000.00		
Taxes	$ 350,000.00	$ 650,000.00	
Rent	$ 48,000.00	$ 602,000.00	
Car(s)	$ 190,000.00	$ 412,000.00	4-5 cars, including one for Mom
Investments	$ 24,000.00	$ 388,000.00	Poor investment habits
Food	$ 50,000.00	$ 338,000.00	
Travel	$ 75,000.00	$ 263,000.00	
Fun	$ 100,000.00	$ 163,000.00	
Legal Fees	$ 25,000.00	$ 138,000.00	
Mom Money	$ 36,000.00	$ 102,000.00	
Family Money	$ 50,000.00	$ 52,000.00	
Furniture	$ 20,000.00	$ 32,000.00	
CPA	$ 4,000.00	$ 28,000.00	
Fin. Advisor	$ 3,000.00	$ 25,000.00	Overpaid for a financial advisor
Misc.	$ 25,000.00	$ -	

D *Is for* Doin' Big Things

D Person [Dee pərsən] ▶ *n.*

1. Structure resembles that of C but lacks any real desire to seek help and looks in the wrong place the few times he does; Fun Friends exceed true friends.

2. Most common responses to those trying to help: "Let me do me. Let me live," and "I made it to this point. I got this."

3. One who lives for the short term, the fun moments to remember, and spends for immediate gratification.

4. Concerns himself mostly with material things, i.e., the hottest girl(s), the latest look, the most luxurious car(s), the shiniest jewelry, and the biggest bottle of Dom Perignon at his own VIP table.

5. Ceases to be concerned with the economic repercussions of his or her actions.

6. Marriage mantra is: the more the merrier—i.e., main girl, side girl(s) but often the side girls get the same treatment as the main girl.

7. Known to alter marriage vow to "till death we live apart;" sees need for more than one place in the same city to accommodate everyone.

Sample Budget: The D Person			
Expenses	Amount	Balance	Notes
New Money	1,000,000.00		
Taxes	$ 350,000.00	$ 650,000.00	
Rent	$ 72,000.00	$ 578,000.00	2 homes
Car(s)	$ 220,000.00	$ 358,000.00	4 cars
Investments	$ -	$ 358,000.00	Terrible investment habits
Food	$ 40,000.00	$ 318,000.00	
Travel	$ 65,000.00	$ 253,000.00	
Fun	$ 95,000.00	$ 158,000.00	
Legal Fees	$ 22,000.00	$ 136,000.00	
Mom Money	$ 30,000.00	$ 106,000.00	
Family Money	$ 50,000.00	$ 56,000.00	
Furniture	$ 50,000.00	$ 6,000.00	
CPA	$ 4,000.00	$ 2,000.00	
Fin. Advisor	$ 2,000.00	$ -	
Misc.	$ -	$ -	

Grades Posted

After reading the previous section, the adolescent and high school scenarios of the test takers become more relevant. Upbringing and environment are critical factors. Where you come from matters, as does whom you surround yourself with later in life, as we've discussed. Where would Student Number 1 and Student Number 2 be if they never met strong mentors to guide them?

If you check in on Number 1 four years from the day she found that money, the shoes and cool clothes she bought at the time are old, too small, and definitely out of style. Student Number 4 has a knowledge base in investing that lasts a lifetime. Number 2 had great intentions but five years later, he was broke because of dishing out money whenever hands were extended. Hopefully, Number 3 continued to seek advice from his best friend's father and others down the line. He probably owns a significant landscaping business (and may have expanded to new neighborhoods) and earns $1,000 or more a week.

If the advice these kids get down the line is poor, if their top fives are weak, they may go downhill; if the advice they absorb is good, and their top fives are strong, they may continue to grow and become wiser. Where you start shapes you, but think of yourself more like clay than concrete—you can continue to mold yourself into who you want to become if you seek out the right advice and follow the right path.

Think about who you would like to become. What grade do you think you earned?

If you believe you deserve an A, you're lucky. The fact that getting an A from the start requires you to be born into a family with excellent resources or a stellar educational base eliminates a lot of people. Is it fair? No, but the reality is that people are born with a certain status and access to resources that puts them ahead of their peers. People who come into money with this status have a harder time losing it because of the support system that has been created since a very young age. Remember, even if you start out as an A, you can still achieve a failing grade.

Anyone who eventually earns a B should be commended for his hard work. This person lacked the foundation that a person earning an A possesses; however, person B worked hard to make sure he sought out the right people to insulate himself from bad decisions. It is possible to earn a B if you learn the lessons and apply them. Much like an A, a B means you have a strong mentorship from the start. Perhaps you anticipated getting money and have already identified the right people that need to be around you when you do. A solid B is not prone to making rash decisions, in part because of the people surrounding him. He's also smart because he learns many lessons through other people's mistakes. If you are not a B, there are lessons to be learned from a B.

If you objectively begin your New Money Millionaire phase with a C, don't despair. You are probably in the majority. I see a C as the most transient grade. You can go either way. Where a person faces criticism is when he has shown no growth or has regressed when it comes time to getting awarded a final grade. A C may tell you that he has goals of growing his money. His goals may align with that of a B; however, he lacks the support and is unable to develop a plan to achieve positive goals. If a person ends up with a C (or lower), he probably didn't apply himself, succumbing to peer pressure. Because of the people that may be around him at times, he runs the risk of falling and becoming a D. Or maybe it's an ego that keeps him from flourishing, refusing to ask for help. He is no better or worse off than when he first signed his contract.

I can easily relate to a C-level person. I signed my contract and then somehow forgot how to put one foot in front of the other. I wanted to do it right, but I didn't have that support in place, so I fell into the D level for most of my first two years in the NFL. The light bulb switched on around my third year. I knew there had to be something better. I didn't feel lost until it hit me that I could be living differently, and then I felt like everything I thought I knew needed to be thrown out the door. Feeling lost was an understatement.

My intentions were always good. I never desired to spend endlessly and live a carefree life. I just fell into it and sought to learn through poor decisions or having too much fun (you might want to call this lifestyle a bad decision). I was a guy who sometimes thought I knew what was best for me, so I would make choices on my own. Fortunately, I didn't settle for a final grade of C or D. I was able to humble myself and own up to the poor decisions I made and not place the blame on others. I found the balance that was lacking for the first two years of my NFL career. I defined myself not by who I was when I entered that New Money Millionaire phase, but who I was when I finished.

In order for a D Person to transition into a C Person and continue to climb, major changes must occur. Additionally, he may find he hits rock bottom before waking from his stupor. This means lifestyle change in a big way, including walking away from all of his Fun Friends and reestablishing real friendships. Unfortunately, this person has been living a lavish existence for so long that when the money dries up, his appearance and his ability to show people that he still has it disappears as well. Those around him believed in who he was when he had money. He doesn't have the same appeal to women. You can learn a lot from a failing person. Look at their mistakes and do not follow them. If you are D, then you need to do a lot in terms of self-examination.

I've noticed that it's a lot easier to find Fun Friends when you're in a position to spend money. It's no different than when you were a child and wanted to go to the friend's house that had the coolest toys. It's more entertaining. Often, when you don't have those things, the women that you thought you had and the friends you thought you had are no longer there. The excitement is lost, not only because the money is gone, but also because you have no one to share your joy with. People remember you, but they remember you for the exciting things, those short-term flings. You become a person used in the past tense, a "used to have it" person. The lesson here is do not become an F.

One more thing you should keep in mind. On each of the sample budgets I've presented, I have included a line for taxes. New Money Millionaires typically do not take into account how much of their earnings go to the government. It's a lot, roughly a third or more, depending on which state you live in. It's not the most exciting thing to talk about. But if you have a good accountant, and you are overpaying during any given year, which is better than underpaying and owing Uncle Sam unexpectedly come April 15ᵗʰ, you will usually get money back. Tax-return money is not spending money; it's getting-ahead money. Around 25 percent of that money should go toward future bills, 50 percent should go toward educational expenses for you and your children, and the remaining quarter can be spent on immediate needs or wants.

The bottom line is this: everyone may start from a different place, but it's where you end up that counts. It's all about advancing, upping your letter grade in life. It starts with money, but then the culture and lifestyle all are stems from that first big paycheck and the choices you make. It's not that hard to understand that people can be handed the same amount of money and all run through it at different speeds. How quickly you learn is up to you. It is all about how you manage the Head-Start Money you are given. Head-Start Money doesn't last forever, nor are you guaranteed a set length of time to live life comfortably.

CHAPTER 11

From Stackin' to Packin':
The Business and Liability of the NFL

I will never forget my game against the Detroit Lions in 2010, when I was playing for the Washington Redskins. There was a short pass to a receiver near my coverage zone. I made the tackle, but one of my teammates fell on me during the play. I could feel that I landed wrong on my hip, but I got up, shook it off, and continued to play. From an early age, athletes learn to play through the pain. You can't advance your career while sitting on the sideline. There's always someone behind you on the depth chart hoping to get your job.

It wasn't until the next year that the MRI showed that I actually had a tear in my right hip. In 2011, I was in a preseason game playing against the Tampa Bay Buccaneers. I was trying to make a tackle, and I could feel my shoulder pop out and back into place (My neck had already started giving me problems that year after breaking up a one-on-one pass during training camp. This resulted in a partial labrum tear to my right shoulder.). The pain on the right side of my body is perpetual; it is with me every day. After my preseason injury, I continued playing until November, when my body just rebelled. It told me that it just couldn't do it anymore. Every time I signed a new contract, I was also signing up for a lifetime of pain.

The *Washington Post* once conducted a survey of retired NFL players. More than 500 players participated. About 85 percent of the players reported receiving five or more major NFL injuries. I was just one of the pack.

From the moment I was seriously injured, I was thrown into the pile of Damaged Goods.

Damaged Goods [da-mij'd gûds] ▸ *n.*

1. One who is no longer seen as valuable to an organization; off-field energy input is greater than on-field energy input.
2. One that can no longer perform on the field at a high level due to injuries or poor decisions off the field.
3. Likely to be labeled, put on sale, and eventually disposed of.
4. Expensive liability with no guarantee of positive results.

As Damaged Goods, I had no choice but to participate rehab. Most damaged goods get thrown in a bin, labeled, and never emerge again. Once I was put on the injured reserve list, or IR, I felt like I was on the brink of being thrown into that bin for good. I started exploring all the options to get my body back to where it needed to be in order to get back on the field. My rehab was extensive and varied. It included stem-cell treatment in the Cayman Islands, against the advice of the Redskins' physicians (About the only treatment that helped me stay on the field, before any major tears to my ligaments, was at the Blast Fitness and Performance Center in Tampa. There, Lynn Olcott gave me Muscle Activation Therapy (MAT), which got me back on the field on a week-to-week basis. But it's only a temporary solution, not a long-term fix for chronic injuries.).

The team doctors seemed to think that I would be fine without surgery. My body was telling me something different. I, too, wasn't completely sold on surgery, so I took it upon myself to exhaust all the alternatives first to avoid going under the knife. This is also standard procedure for non-athletes where elective surgery is an option. A good surgeon will tell you, "I'm your last stop, after you exhaust all the other alternatives."

It is standard procedure at the end of a season to have an exit physical, where you are examined by doctors, followed by a sign-off on your end, claiming that you are healthy and ready to play the next season. It is especially important for a team to have a player entering free agency to sign off, because it takes the liability off the team. Initially, I didn't sign it because I didn't feel the same way I usually do after a season of playing. I just wasn't right.

The conversations with the trainer and team doctor were standard. "How do you feel?" they'd ask. I would answer, "I don't feel confident enough that my body is okay to sign off." Until I signed off, the Redskins were still responsible for my physical health. The trainer kept nagging me to sign off and presented it as the only way to reap the benefits when I became a free agent. The phone calls became extremely aggravating. Every time, however, I gave the same response: "I'm not feeling able to play or work out in the normal way that I'm used to in the off-season." The bottom line was, I was Damaged Goods, and they were trying to get me off their liability list.

The deadline for me to sign off and begin free agency was quickly approaching, so I flew to Washington, DC to meet with the team doctor. He said, "We're trying to make sure you feel good." But then, at the end of the conversation, I could expect a statement like, "We just want to make sure you feel good for free agency."

The biggest mistake I made was signing the paperwork. I had doubts about my injuries, but I also knew that I had played through pain in the past. I was optimistic that it would get better, per the advice of the team doctor. For some reason, it didn't hit me that I had been doing rehab for the past nine months and nothing had changed. I think a part of it was denial. I was really hurt and holding onto a small hope that one day I would wake up and feel like myself again. I also think the other part was that the doctors worked for the team, not me.

The pain was excruciating, and the therapy, medicine, and treatments were no help. Thus, I was left with one last hope: surgical repair. But by signing off, I started a battle with the NFL over who should pay for my surgery.

I even tried Regenokine and traveled to a specialist in New York to get it. This therapy is part of a larger category of treatments known as "biologic medicine," in which your own tissues are extracted, carefully manipulated, and then reintroduced into your body (The list of people who have also experimented with Regenokine reportedly includes Kobe Bryant, Fred Couples, Hollywood talent agent Ari Emanuel and the late Pope John Paul II.). I learned later that the Regenokine treatment does not help repair torn labrums. So I was out of pocket for $22,000 plus airfare and hotels in New York while I stayed there for five days.

Despite my faith in these treatments, my body was still telling me something wasn't right.

I am still getting inquiries daily on social-media websites, or in passing, asking me why I am not playing. My response is, I'm still fighting injuries. There were teams calling to ask me to try out, and despite me being prepared mentally, I wasn't prepared physically. I knew that I wouldn't be able to go to a tryout and show that I was physically capable. My body was talking louder than the teams interested in my services. Unfortunately, teams could beg for me to come try out but assume no liability for me being healthy enough to play. That wasn't their job.

Since I am no longer attached to a team, the process of recovering from a major injury is entirely different. It's slow. The Redskins are doing whatever they can to delay, in hopes that I will give up on trying to get them to pay for the operation, as would any team (The battle between worker's compensation and the Redskins was more about lifetime treatment, should I need it. If I had paid for the surgery—which I certainly could have afforded—then I would not get any long-term benefits. It is an open secret that the NFL has among the worst benefits package of any professional sport. But the players realize that something is better than nothing).

It's interesting—but not entirely surprising—that an organization that once fought on my behalf is now fighting against me . . . an organization that had personnel in place to make sure I was taken care of on and off the field. Finally, after a lot of back-and-forth, I won my case and had hip surgery from a torn labrum in my right hip on August 12, 2013.

Things are moving in the right direction.

CHAPTER 12

Conclusion:
Your Postgame Strategy

NFL Gratitude to Next-Level Altitude

I've referenced the word "success" many times throughout this book. It's a word I feel that you can't repeat too many times. Success is a journey, something you set out to accomplish. Once you find success, it is time to redefine your journey.

My advice? Put away the scrapbook for your children and grandchildren to peruse someday. Forget the great games you had where your name was in the next day's headlines. Forget all those slaps on the back you got on the sidelines from those people you didn't know who wished you well.

Here's a quote to think about: "For over a thousand years Roman conquerors returning from the wars enjoyed the honor of triumph, a tumultuous parade. In the procession came trumpeters, musicians and strange animals from conquered territories, together with carts laden with treasure and captured armaments. The conquerors rode in a triumphal chariot, the dazed prisoners walking in chains before him. Sometimes his children robed in white stood with him in the chariot or rode the racehorses. A slave stood behind the conqueror holding a golden crown and whispered in his ear a warning: all glory is fleeting." That's from a speech General George S. Patton gave more than half a century ago.

Life goals are always looming. Every day is a challenge. Every day is an opportunity. You can waste it or do something with it.

If you learn anything at all from this book, let it be this: don't bask in past successes. By definition "bask" means to lounge or relax. Basking is for the lazy. It creates a state of complacency, making it easy to fall into oblivion. By deciding you have a life after your initial flush of wealth, you are eschewing the trappings of complacent living. Complacency is just another word for a slow death.

Success is something you need to personally define—a definition that has to make you hungry and sets you down a path to achieve something that will better you and others. Once you are there, get to a point where you can redefine your definition. Up the ante. There will be obstacles to overcome and some may experience more obstacles than others depending on individual circumstances.

But be clear about this: your definition of success at nineteen should not be the same definition of success at age twenty-five or thirty-two. When I was eighteen, I defined success as earning a full athletic scholarship to a Division I institution for football. At age twenty-five, success meant being able to maintain my million-dollar status. Now at age thirty-two, success is finding other sources of income and thereby maintaining the comfortable lifestyle I had established from the Head-Start Money. I am constantly redefining what it means for me to succeed.

It's all part of your Postgame.

As you can easily guess, my New Money Millionaire stage is so far behind me I don't give it any serious thought. Now, in my Postgame, I'm working on a graphic novel, *The Supernals Experiment*, which I hope to turn into a film. I also have other novels in the works. You can check them out on my website: octocanon.com, which is a comprehensive hub for many of my business ventures. In addition, I am also releasing a children's book series on managing money, titled: *Little Phil's Financial Education Series*. So far there are four books in the series: *Little Phil's New Money Friends*, *Little Phil's Piggy Bank*, *Jenny meets Penny*, and *Little Phil's Family Finances*. Moreover, I'm planning to release a board game, also called New Money, in conjunction with this book. If you liked Monopoly at some point in your life, then you will find this game even more compelling.

Today, I am on my way to becoming a Self-Made Millionaire. I am getting ready to launch Tappish, a social-media website that creates intimate connections between consumers and their respective markets, as well as between businesses and their potential customers—an idea that came to me years ago while on the road for an away game.

Maybe it's time for you to redefine success. Once you do, create a plan and seek out people; hopefully your top five will help you execute that plan.

I cannot overemphasize the fact that I refuse to be defined by the success I had on the football field alone. I'm a big believer in using your first success to explore other avenues toward further and higher forms of success. I am forever grateful for the opportunities football has given me. I can now explore new avenues that will ultimately redefine what success means to me.

I've done my homework. I went back and finished my degree at the University of Miami. Some people told me I had enough money not to have to go back to school, but for me it was absolutely necessary. That college degree was right for me. I walked away with relationships with professors that will support me in my future. I enrolled in more classes in the NFL's Business Management and Entrepreneurship Program. I enrolled in the NFL's Hollywood Boot Camp (it was a crash course on the different components of filmmaking). I also attended the NFL Consumer Product Boot Camp.

I'm no longer defined by being an athlete. I'm a college graduate. Someday, I want my kids to know that they should be proudest of me as a father and a provider. What has defined you? If it's the same thing that you have been defined by since your training phase, then I recommend redefining yourself by first redefining your definition of success. Success must be seen as a constant evolution.

Keep this in the forefront of your mind: One poor decision can turn your world upside down. One poor decision can cost you your career, livelihood, or even your life. Some people are able to bounce back, and some are not. The saying, "You are not defined by a situation; rather, by how you respond" is true. I think of Ray Lewis, who happened to be in the wrong place at the wrong time. For years, Ray was an accused murderer, but Ray has proven to be one of the most resilient people out there. The following year he was named the Super Bowl MVP. He has become a powerful voice of inspiration.

Donte Stallworth drove home while intoxicated after a fun night at a Miami club and killed a pedestrian crossing the causeway. Donte paid the consequences and refocused on his career. While it's a decision he will never forget, the only thing it has dictated is better decisions in his future.

Michael Vick faced a lot of public scrutiny for his now infamous dog-fighting incident; however, he faced the consequences, persevered, and was awarded another opportunity to play football. Vick was humbled by the experience. He knew he was wrong; he paid the penalty. He came back. He's a better person for it, and the public who berated him now gives him props. We are a forgiving society. Americans love stories about redemption. If you screw up, you can redeem yourself. That's the lesson from Michael Vick.

Not everyone copes as well. Rae Carruth, another NFL football player, is behind bars, and it all boils down to him getting a woman pregnant. The woman went against his wishes to abort the baby, so he put a hit out on her. She was murdered, but the baby lived. What a mess. Carruth has until approximately 2018 to think about ways he can redeem himself when he reenters society.

Aaron Hernandez is another ex–football player in trouble. In 2013, he was indicted by a grand jury for murder and is currently being investigated in connection with other murders in Massachusetts. Hernandez maintains his innocence, but the court of public opinion already has taken a dim view of his case.

As a pro football player—any person in a position of wealth or celebrity—you are vulnerable to bad things happening. Sometimes you make bad decisions that are so small, so minute, you don't even know you're making them. Maybe it has to do with the company you are keeping. All it takes is somebody making an innocent remark and personal information may leak to the wrong person. For example, somebody found out that my friend Sean Taylor kept cash in his house. An outstanding safety for the University of Miami and the Washington Redskins, Taylor was accidentally killed during a home robbery in 2007. I knew him as a teammate in college, and he was very humble and driven. Unfortunately, he was shot in his home while his house was ransacked and his longtime girlfriend cowered under his bed with their eighteen-month-old daughter. He died later at the hospital, just twenty-four years old. Now that's a tragedy. Was it his fault? Of course not. But he's no longer here with us today.

I have been in plenty of situations where it was easier to make the wrong decision. Sometimes it's harder to do what is undoubtedly right.

This is just the tip of the iceberg for me. I write this book from the heart. I don't know if I'm really at the point of arrival, but many people—especially other athletes, my peers, who have lost their way—would love to be in the position that I'm currently in. Imagine being a millionaire with the great potential of multiplying my fortune because I have planted a lot of seeds, put in the hard work, and continued to make smarter moves.

Although I sleep and walk with pain from my NFL injuries day in and day out, I still feel good because I get the chills from my late nights of brainstorming and writing at 3:00 in the morning, when much of the world is still asleep. It's the same as going on a late-night jog in high school while everybody was doing teenage things.

I'm eating a slice of pizza from my favorite pizza joint in Miami—Andiamo. Then a quick flashback hits me. I'm back in Ft. Myers at Lee Middle School in the eighth grade. I'm sitting in class with some of my Pop Warner teammates for the Riverdale Wildcats. The morning news always previewed a song, and that morning the intercom introduced me to Warren G: "You don't see what I see every day as Warren G and you don't hear what I hear." At that time, I didn't totally understand the lyrics, but somehow they resonated. Those words allowed me to dream big. I wanted to see what Warren G saw. I knew I was destined for something big in football or baseball, but I was also confident I was destined for greatness in life. So as the tune in Warren G's song plays in my head right now, I'm here firing in multiple lanes, not just football and baseball, but life.

If this were a chess game, my next few moves would lead straight to a checkmate. If you're feeling like someone else is about to checkmate you, if you're feeling lost, it's okay. It takes awhile to get the hang of the game. So, look up and link up with people who know their purpose and, in turn, they can help you figure out your purpose. Do your homework; the right mentor is everything—someone who can really help steer you in the right direction.

Whatever you do, don't put limits on goals—the more you dream, the further you will go.

Appendix

This is the cheat sheet, takeaways on the most important themes I talked about in this book.

1. Nobody will care about your finances more than you do.
2. The money might be great right now, but if you're not careful, it's not going to last forever (Reread number 1).
3. When you're new to things, you do stupid things. Realize this going in, and wise up fast.
4. New money is like a newborn baby: it doesn't come with an instruction manual. You have to write your own.
5. While the Self-Made Millionaires were calculating how to grow their money, I was calculating how to spend my money. The sooner you learn this is a bad plan, the better.
6. It became clear that the majority of New Money Millionaires were spending as blindly as I was. These are not the people from whom you want advice. When you're out there as a New Money Millionaire, find someone with 20/20 vision.
7. Every lesson is a blessin'. Why? We learn more from our mistakes than from our successes. Try not to repeat a mistake.
8. Start competing to be on top, financially—be the one who saved the most, the one that has more assets than liabilities, and the one who has identified the best mentor.
9. Watch those that are in faster lanes than yours, and let them inspire you. Just don't jump into their lane too fast.
10. You can walk away with at least one important thing from every conversation you have. Listen more, talk less.
11. Historical Friends aren't always your true friends.

12. Mentors should stress the importance of doing things right, not right now.

13. Don't invest until you have solid mentorship, solid business partnerships, and a solid vision.

14. Don't be afraid to ask questions when you do not know the answer. When you are learning, there is no such thing as a stupid question.

15. Commercial and investment banks are just as capable of helping pay your bills as is a financial advisor.

16. Poor company corrupts good character. Avoid bad influences.

17. Your friends play a role in your ultimate success; choose them wisely.

18. Head-Start Money doesn't last forever, nor are you guaranteed a set length of time to live life comfortably. It's up to you to make it happen.

19. Every time you sign a contract, ask yourself if you are also signing yourself up for a lifetime of pain.

20. You must constantly retrain your mind for your next achievement and life pursuit. Ignite your postgame.

21. When you have learned enough life lessons, pass them on to your siblings and your children.

ACKNOWLEDGMENTS

I've had a lot of input and advice in my life, and it continued as I wrote this book. I would like to thank Kelly Pierce, Jonathan Nash, Tavares Felton, Darien Smith, Wilfred Rivera, Nick Monsanto, Andre Monsanto, George Wilson, the late Sylvester Goran, Ellen M. McPhillip, Gary Shiffman, Michelle White, Kim Mcglohon, Mary Buchanon, Robert Plant, the late Al Davis, Billy Corben, the Adame family, Virginia Gonzales, Adrienne Carman, Susan Wright, Brenda Pannell, Edgerrin James, Bruce Allen, Chuck Pagano, Jon Gruden, Paul Kelly, Rawheem Morris, Ronde Barber, Ryan Nece, Rod Woodson, Tim Brown, Jerry Rice, Derrick Brooks, London Fletcher, John Lynch and David Buehrer, and my family (both those who have supported me and those who gave me substance for this book).

I especially appreciate John Singleton, whose movie *Boys in the Hood* motivated me to move my life in a positive direction. Thank you also to Plies, Earnest Graham, Jevon Kearse, Tim Bursey, Joe Williams, Larry Gary, Big Gates, the Shiffman family, Butch Davis, Greg Schiano, Randy Shannon, Amy Deem, Eric Campbell, Lonny Bereal, the University of Miami, the 2001 University of Miami National Championship football team, and the NFL.

Finally, I'd like to also express my appreciation to two athletes that inspired me all my life—Bo Jackson and Deion Sanders, as well as the motivational speaker Eric Thomas. I'm grateful for all of my experiences, good and bad, for making me the person I am today.